more

DATA HANDLING

more

DATA HANDLING

For National Curriculum levels 2–5

SPECTRUM MATHS

Dave Kirkby

UNWIN HYMAN

Published in 1990 by
UNWIN HYMAN LIMITED
15/17 Broadwick Street
London W1V 1FP

British Library Cataloguing in Publication Data
Kirkby, Dave
Spectrum mathematics.
More data handling
1. Mathematics
I. Title II. Series
510

ISBN 0 04 448199 3

Designed and illustrated by AMR, Basingstoke
Printed in Great Britain by The Alden Press Ltd, Oxford
Bound by Hunter & Foulis Ltd, Edinburgh

Contents

Introduction

Most schools use a mathematics scheme or schemes to teach basic skills and concepts, but teachers still require a wide range of materials to supplement these schemes. Such materials are provided by the **Spectrum Maths** series.

This is a series of three books of data handling activities primarily for the primary years, although secondary school teachers with low attaining pupils will also find these books useful.

They are defined in terms of three ability levels.

Starting Data Handling – for National Curriculum levels 1–3
More Data Handling – for National Curriculum levels 2–5
Go Further with Data Handling – for National Curriculum levels 3–6

Each book contains 40 data handling activities in the form of:

- a photocopiable pupil sheet
- detailed teacher's notes about the mathematical content and objectives, the apparatus required, activities for the pupils, and examples of questions to be asked of the pupils.

The National Curriculum in Mathematics has devoted three of its 14 Attainment Targets to Data Handling. Namely:

> AT 12: Pupils should collect, record and process data.
> AT 13: Pupils should represent and interpret data.
> AT 14: Pupils should understand estimate and calculate probabilities.

Spectrum Maths Data Handling should prove an invaluable resource for pupils and teachers in meeting the needs and requirements of the data handling elements of the National Curriculum.

Although the main focus of the material is data handling, many of the activities will naturally involve other aspects of the National Curriculum. Particularly prominent is:

AT 9: Using and applying mathematics.

The **Cockcroft Report** also emphasises the importance of data handling:

> 'Throughout the primary years attention should be paid to methods of presenting mathematical information in pictorial and graphical form, and also to interpreting information which is presented in this way. It can often be the case that graphical work lacks variety and progression, so that older children are limited to drawing graphs which differ little from those which are to be found in infant classrooms. Children need experience of a wide variety of graphical work; the mere drawing of graphs should not be over-emphasised. It is essential to discuss and interpret the information which is displayed both in graphs which children have themselves drawn and also in graphs which they have not.'
>
> [**Cockcroft Report**: *Mathematics Counts* paragraph 293]

This series does not claim to be a fully comprehensive coverage of all aspects of data handling. The format of photocopiable material accompanied by detailed teacher's notes is not appropriate, for example, for computer use.

Using the pupils' sheets

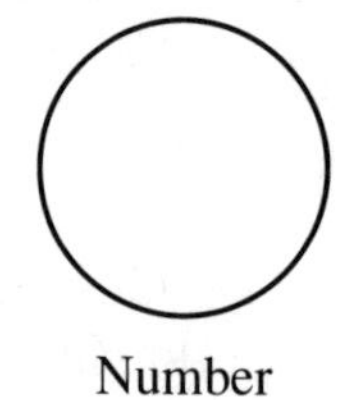

The **pupil sheets** take the form of either:

a **data source,**

or **data representation.**

These are both used for providing children with experiences in the collection and analysis of data.

Using the teacher's notes

Main focus of the data handling activity

Brief outline of the mathematical content and purpose of the activity.

Apparatus

Description of any apparatus required.

Activity

Children may need to perform some activity based on the pupil sheet before they are ready for the suggested 'sample activities'. This section outlines such activities.

LEVEL	Profile Component 1				Profile Component 2		
	UA	N	A	M	UA	S	D
1							
2							
3							
4							
5							
6							
7							
8							
9							
10							

KEY UA Using and Applying Mathematics
N Number
A Algebra
M Measures
S Shape and Space
D Handling Data

The teacher's notes for each activity contain the above table. This table refers to the attainment targets and levels of the National Curriculum. An attempt has been made to locate, by means of dots in the table, the approximate content level for each activity but it must be appreciated that many activities can be performed at a variety of different levels.

Handling the data – sample activities

This section contains examples of activities for children using the pupil sheet as a starting point. It is assumed that the teacher will discuss activities with the pupils and lead them appropriately. The notes highlight particular components of data handling, namely, the ability to

collect data
record data
process data
represent data
interpret data

In some cases particular activities may embody all of these components, leading pupils towards the more general **'using and applying mathematics'.**

Interpreting the data – sample questions

It is most important that pupils are given experiences in interpreting data and its representation. This section provides some examples for the teacher of questions he/she might ask in order to provide pupils with such experiences. Pupils are given further experiences in interpreting data when asked to write sentences about specific data and its representation.

1 Attendances

Bar Graphs

Data Collection

Interpreting a bar graph showing the attendance figures for a given class for one week. Drawing similar graphs to illustrate the figures for your own class.

LEVEL	Profile Component 1				Profile Component 2		
	UA	N	A	M	UA	S	D
1							
2		●			●		
3					●		●
4					●		
5							
6							
7							
8							
9							
10							

N2 Ordering two-digit numbers.
D3 Bar graph.

Handling the data – sample activities

- **Collect data** based on the class' attendances over a period of a week. Draw a bar graph to illustrate the data (**represent data**). Write some sentences about the graph (**interpret data**).
- Monitor the attendance figures over a longer period, a term for example, and record on a bar chart on the wall (**collect, record, represent data**).
- **Collect data** from other classes. Analyse and compare the data (**using and applying**).

Interpreting the data – sample questions

- How many children are there in class on Monday, Tuesday,...?
- On which day were there most children in class? Which had the fewest?
- How many absences on Friday, Thursday,...?
- How many more children in class on Wednesday than Thursday, Tuesday than Monday, ...?
- How many absences altogether on Monday and Tuesday?
- Why do you think there were so many absences on Friday?

Attendances

Write some sentences about this graph.

2 Best for me

Lists

Data collection

Completing a data collection sheet showing preferences for different things. Using several of these as a data base from which to select information and analyse it.

LEVEL	Profile Component 1				Profile Component 2		
	UA	N	A	M	UA	S	D
1							
2					●		●
3					●		●
4					●		
5							
6							
7							
8							
9							
10							

D2 Data collection sheets.
D3 Data bases. Lists.

Handling the data – sample activities

- Pin up the responses on the wall for a class and, in groups, choose a particular category, and **collect data**. For example, one group could look through the sheets and collect all the responses to 'Best TV programmes'. These could be listed (**record data**) and then a table constructed to condense the information (**process data**). Then a graph can be drawn to illustrate the information (**represent data**).
- Design your own 'BEST FOR ME' sheet but choosing different categories. **Collect data** by asking pupils to complete the sheet. Analyse the data (**using and applying**).

Interpreting the data – sample questions

- What is your 'Best song'? What would be your second best?
- Which did you find difficult to choose?
- Who chose red for 'Best colour'? What other choices have people made?
- What choices could you make for 'Best sport'?

Best for me

2

Best male singer ....

Best female singer ....

Best song ....

Best food ....

Best drink ....

Best TV programmes ....

Best book ....

Best sport ....

Best colours ....

Best sweets ....

Best toy ....

Complete the sheet. Find a partner who has also completed the sheet and compare the results.

3 Babes in the wood

Lists

Reading and interpreting the list of performances for a pantomime.

LEVEL	Profile Component 1				Profile Component 2		
	UA	N	A	M	UA	S	D
1							
2							
3				●			●
4							
5							
6							
7							
8							
9							
10							

M3 Reading and interpreting dates and times.
D3 Reading lists.

Handling the data – sample activities

- Find some programmes from a nearby theatre and analyse the number and times of performances (**process, interpret data**).

Interpreting the data – sample questions

- When does the pantomime start? When does it finish?
- How many Saturdays does the pantomime play for?
- How many performances are there each day?
- What time do the performances start on Friday 15 December, Monday 4 December, ...?
- On what dates is the first performance at 10.00?
- On what dates is the second performance at 2.30?
- How many performances are there in the first week, second week, ...?
- How many performances are there in January, in November?
- How many days off do the cast have at Christmas?
- How many days does the pantomime play altogether?
- How many school matinees are there?

Babes in the wood

by Jack Lee and Mary Evans

Summerfield Theatre,
Swan Street,
Sheffield
S1 1DA

Performance Schedule

Wed	29 Nov	2.30(p)	7.00(p)
Thur	30 Nov	2.30(p)	7.00
Fri	1 Dec	2.30*	7.00
Sat	2 Dec	2.30	7.00
Mon	4 Dec	2.30*	7.00
Tues	5 Dec	10.00*	2.30*
Wed	6 Dec	2.30*	7.00
Thur	7 Dec	10.00*	2.30*
Fri	8 Dec	2.30*	7.00
Sat	9 Dec	2.30*	7.00
Mon	11 Dec	2.30*	7.00
Tues	12 Dec	10.00*	2.30*
Wed	13 Dec	2.30*	7.00
Thur	14 Dec	2.30*	7.00
Fri	15 Dec	2.30*	7.00
Sat	16 Dec	2.30+	7.00
Mon	18 Dec	2.30	7.00
Tues	19 Dec	2.30	7.00
Wed	20 Dec	2.30	7.00
Thur	21 Dec	2.30	7.00
Fri	22 Dec	2.30	7.00+
Sat	23 Dec	2.30+	7.00+
Tues	26 Dec	2.30+	7.00+
Wed	27 Dec	2.30+	7.00+
Thur	28 Dec	2.30+	7.00+
Fri	29 Dec	2.30+	7.00+
Sat	30 Dec	2.30+	7.00+
Mon	1 Jan	2.30+	7.00+
Tues	2 Jan	2.30	7.00
Wed	3 Jan	2.30	7.00
Thur	4 Jan	2.30	7.00
Fri	5 Jan	2.30	7.00
Sat	6 Jan	2.30+	7.00
Mon	8 Jan	2.30*	7.00
Tues	9 Jan	2.30*	7.00
Wed	10 Jan	2.30*	7.00
Thur	11 Jan	2.30*	7.00
Fri	12 Jan	2.30*	7.00
Sat	13 Jan	2.30+	7.00

(p) Previews * School matinees
+ No concessions

Thursday 30 November 1989

Saturday 13 January 1990

The traditional family pantomime... A magical adventure story with music and laughter, spectacular effects, fabulous costumes.

Write some sentences about this list.

more DATA HANDLING SPECTRUM MATHS

4 Brothers and sisters

Frequency tables
Bar graphs
Bar line graphs
Data collection

Collecting data on the total numbers of brothers and sisters for each pupil in the class. Constructing a frequency table.

LEVEL	Profile Component 1				Profile Component 2		
	UA	N	A	M	UA	S	D
1							
2					●		●
3					●		●
4					●		●
5							
6							
7							
8							
9							
10							

D2 Frequency table.
D3 Bar graph.
D4 Bar line graph.

Activity

Pupils write the names of each member of the class in the table, and then record, alongside these, the total number of brothers and sisters for each pupil.

Handling the data – sample activities

- Draw a bar graph or bar line graph to represent the data (**represent data**).

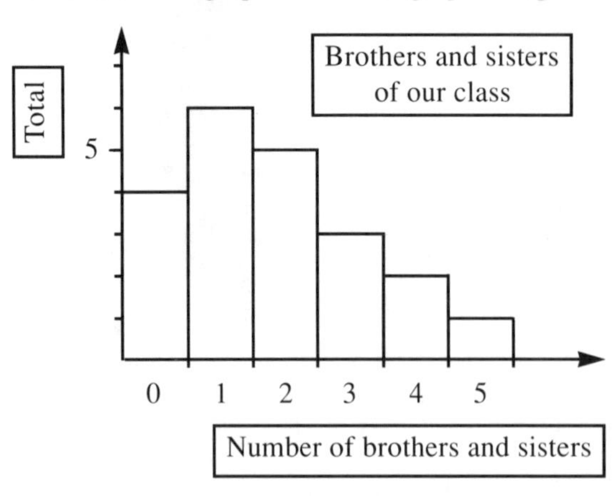

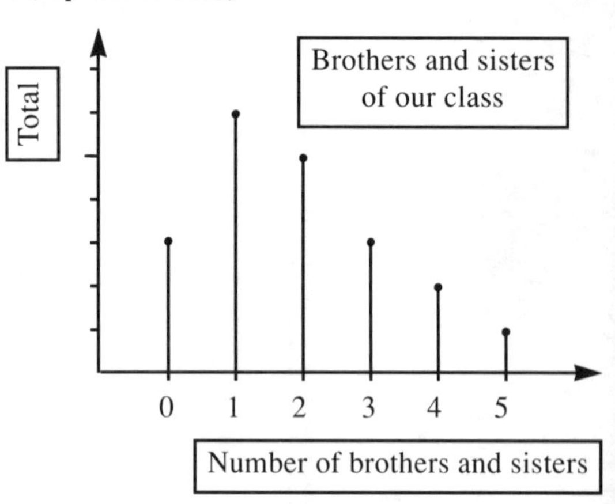

- **Collect data** for another class and compare (**record, process, represent data**).
- **Collect data** for (a) brothers only (b) sisters only, then compare (**record, process, represent, interpret data**).
- Find the average number of brothers and sisters for the class (**process data**).

Interpreting the data – sample questions

- Who has the most brothers and sisters?
- Who has three, one, ...?
- How many brothers and sisters does ____ have?
- How many of the pupils have two brothers or sisters?
- How many have more than two brothers or sisters?
- How many more brothers or sisters does ____ have than ____?
- How many brothers and sisters between the whole class?

Brothers and sisters

4

Name	Brothers and sisters	Name	Brothers and sisters	Name	Brothers and sisters

Number of brothers and sisters		Total
0 1 2 3 4 5		

Name	Brothers and sisters
John	3
Sita	0
Gary	1

Number of brothers and sisters		Total
0	~~llll~~ l	
1	ll	
2	lll	

more DATA HANDLING SPECTRUM MATHS

5 Opening times

Tables

Bar graphs

Data collection

Analysing the opening hours for different shops. Calculating the number of hours the shops are open, and drawing bar graphs to illustrate the data. Collecting data from local shops.

LEVEL	Profile Component 1				Profile Component 2		
	UA	N	A	M	UA	S	D
1							
2							
3		●		●			●
4		●					
5							
6							
7							
8							
9							
10							

N3/N4 Number problems involving times.
M3 Reading and interpreting time.
D3 Tables. Bar graphs.

Handling the data – sample activities

- Draw a table to show the number of hours open for (a) the sweet shop, (b) the fish and chip shop (**process data**).
- Then draw bar graphs to show the number of hours each shop is open for each day of the week (**represent data**).
- Write some sentences about the two graphs (**interpret data**).
- **Collect data** from local shops on opening times and analyse and compare them.

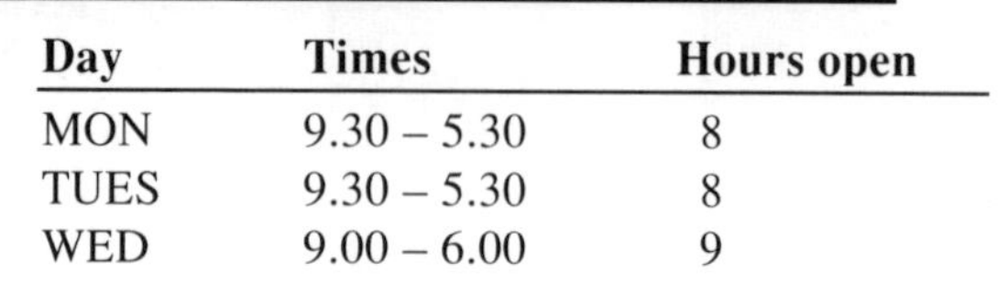

Day	Times	Hours open
MON	9.30 – 5.30	8
TUES	9.30 – 5.30	8
WED	9.00 – 6.00	9

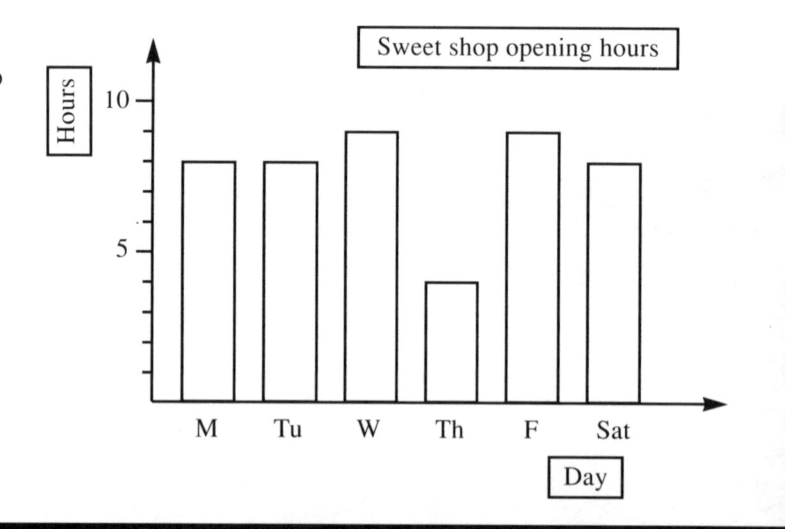

Interpreting the data – sample questions

- When is the sweet shop open on Tuesdays, Fridays, ...?
- What time does the fish and chip shop close on Tuesdays, Fridays, ...?
- When is the sweetshop's afternoon closing? What about the fish and chip shop?
- How many hours is the fish and chip shop open on Mondays, Thursdays, ...?
- Which is the longest day for the sweet shop owner? What about the fish and chip shop owner?
- How many hours is each shop open in a week?

Opening times

SWEETS

OPENING TIMES

Mon	9.30 am – 5.30 pm
Tues	9.30 am – 5.30 pm
Wed	9.00 am – 6.00 pm
Thur	9.00 am – 1.00 pm
Fri	9.00 am – 6.00 pm
Sat	9.00 am – 5.00 pm

FISH AND CHIPS

OPEN

Mon	5.00 pm – 11.00 pm
Tues	5.00 pm – 11.00 pm
Wed	CLOSED
Thur	5.30 pm – 10.30 pm
Fri	5.00 pm – 11.30 pm
Sat	11.30 am – 3.00 pm
	5.30 pm – 11.00 pm

6 Pop charts

Lists

Studying pop charts, and comparing movement of the position of records based on data given for two consecutive weeks.

LEVEL	Profile Component 1				Profile Component 2		
	UA	N	A	M	UA	S	D
1							
2					●		
3		●			●		●
4					●		
5							
6							
7							
8							
9							
10							

N3 introducing negative numbers.
D3 Lists.

Handling the data – sample activities

- Write alongside each record a measure of its progress from last week to this week, e.g. ‘UP 3’ or ‘DOWN 2’ (**process data**).
- Use ‘+’ notation for ‘UP’ and ‘–’ notation for ‘DOWN’.
- **Collect data** from current pop charts and analyse in the same way.
- **Collect data** weekly over many weeks, monitor progress and analyse (**using and applying**).

Interpreting the data – sample questions

- Which record is fifth, eighth, ...?
- What position is ‘The Stare’, ‘Crazy baby’, ...?
- Who sings ‘Burning’, ...?
- What position was ‘Instant playback’, ‘Golden sunset’. ... last week?
- Has ‘Birthday present’ gone up or down since last week? By how much?
- Which record is number 1? Which was number 1 last week?
- Which record has gone up three places, down one place, ...?
- How many records have gone up, how many down?

Pop charts

TOP OF THE POPS

☆NEW ENTRY

Last week	This week		
(2)	1	HEART TO HEART	KIM JACKSON
(1)	2	LONG LASTING LOVE	THE KING
☆	3	IT'S MINE	CLAUDETTE
(5)	4	BURNING	PHIL JAMES
(7)	5	CRAZY BABY	THE BEATS
(9)	6	SILVER ON THE CLOUD	THE DAMIAN BOYS
(28)	7	GOLDEN SUNSET	KOO KOO
(23)	8	NOTHING LOOKS LIKE YOU	GINO
(4)	9	BIRTHDAY PRESENT	DAVID STANSFIELD
(6)	10	THE STARE	PEACEMAKERS
(8)	11	ALL OVER AGAIN	GLASGOW GIRLS
(3)	12	PILLOW DREAMS	THE TUESDAYS
(16)	13	INSTANT PLAYBACK	FRED STEVEN
(26)	14	JUST LIKE ME	NIGEL SMITH
(21)	15	COULD HAVE LIED	SARA-ANN
(17)	16	BABY LOVE	NIGHTSINGERS
(10)	17	RED VELVET	LOOP
(18)	18	SALLIE	INSPIRED CARPETS
(13)	19	DEEP IN LOVE WITH YOU	YELL
(14)	20	RAINING TEARS	GOLDEN ARROW

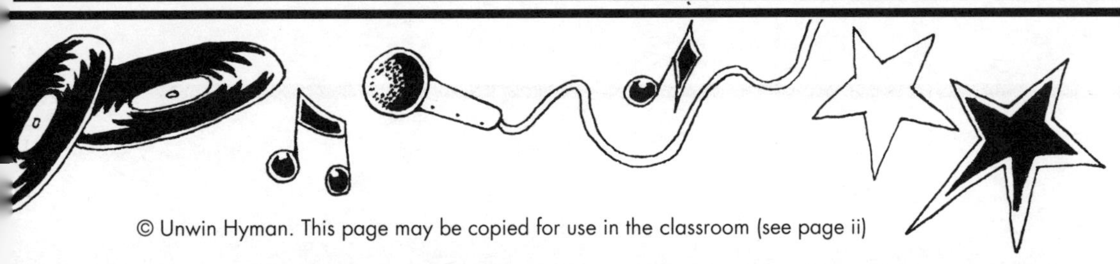

7 TV programmes

Tables

Bar graphs

Analysing the times of television programmes. Calculation of the length of time for each programme and making comparisons between them. Drawing tables and bar graphs to illustrate the results.

LEVEL	Profile Component 1				Profile Component 2		
	UA	N	A	M	UA	S	D
1							
2					●		
3				●	●		●
4					●		
5							
6							
7							
8							
9							
10							

M3 Problems associated with time.
D3 Bar graphs. Tables.

Handling the data – sample activities

- Construct a table to show how long each programme lasts (**process data**). Draw a bar graph to illustrate the length of each programme (**represent data**). Write some sentences about the graph (**interpret data**).

Programme	Start	Finish	Time
Laurel and Hardy	3.50	4.00	10 mins
Spider Hunt	4.00	4.10	10 mins
Mysterious Cities	4.10	4.35	25 mins

- Cut out the television programmes from a current newspaper and analyse the programme lengths (**using and applying**).

Interpreting the data – sample questions

- Which programme starts at 5.35, 9.00, ...?
- Which programme finishes at 8.15, 11.20, ...?
- Which programme follows after 'Laurel and Hardy', ...?
- How long does 'Back Chat', 'Weather', ... last?
- Which programmes last for more than 30 minutes, less than 30 minutes?
- How many programmes could you watch between 4 o'clock and 6 o'clock?
- How long do the films last?
- When are the news programmes?
- How much time is devoted to News?
- How long will it take to watch 'Back Chat' and 'Time for a Change'?

TV programmes

3.50 **LAUREL AND HARDY** (repeat).
4.00 **SPIDER HUNT.**
4.10 **MYSTERIOUS CITIES OF GOLD** (repeat).
4.35 **A HITCH IN TIME:** Inside the ruins of an old castle, an eccentric professor is testing out a new time machine. It keeps going wrong, so he invites two children to become his assistants and help with the tests. They get some curious and unexpected results.
5.35 **ACACIA ROAD.**
6.00 **NEWS; WEATHER.**
6.30 **LOOK NORTH.**
7.00 **BACK CHAT.** Guests include tenor Luciano Pavarotti, Inner Space star Martin Short and funny girl Sandra Dickinson, with music from Bristol Beat.
7.40 **TIME FOR A CHANGE.** Hosted by Chris Blake.
8.15 **DREAM TIME.**
9.00 **NEWS; WEATHER.**
9.30 **FILM: MAD COW.**
11.20 **INTERNATIONAL TENNIS:** Highlights of the quarter-finals in the Stella Artois Championship at Queen's Club, London.
12.10 **FILM: DOUBLE VISION.**
1.30 **WEATHER.**
1.35 **CLOSE.**

How long does each programme last?

8 Burgers

Lists

Bar line graphs

Interpretation of a menu showing different types of burgers at two weights, together with their prices. Drawing bar line graphs to illustrate the differences in prices between the types.

LEVEL	Profile Component 1				Profile Component 2		
	UA	N	A	M	UA	S	D
1							
2							
3		●		●			●
4							●
5							
6							
7							
8							
9							
10							

N3/M4 Problems involving money.
D3 Lists.
D4 Bar line graphs.

Handling the data – sample activities

- Collect menus from local eating houses and discuss/compare/analyse the prices (**interpret data**).
- Draw a bar line graph to show the differences in prices between the various 1/4 lb burgers (**represent data**). Write about it (**interpret data**).
- Draw bar line graphs to show the differences in prices between 1/4 lb and 1/2 lb burgers (**represent data**).

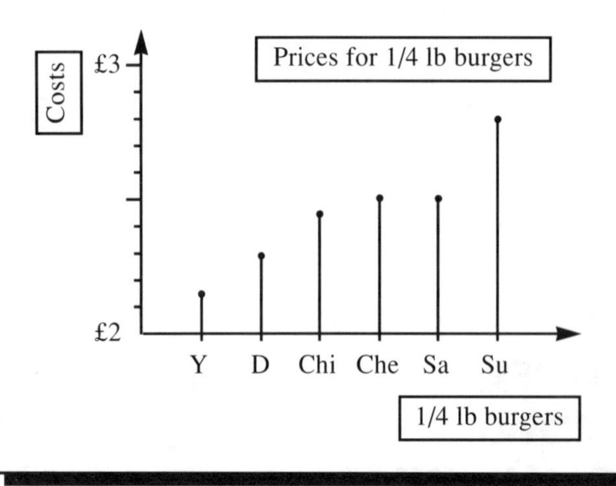

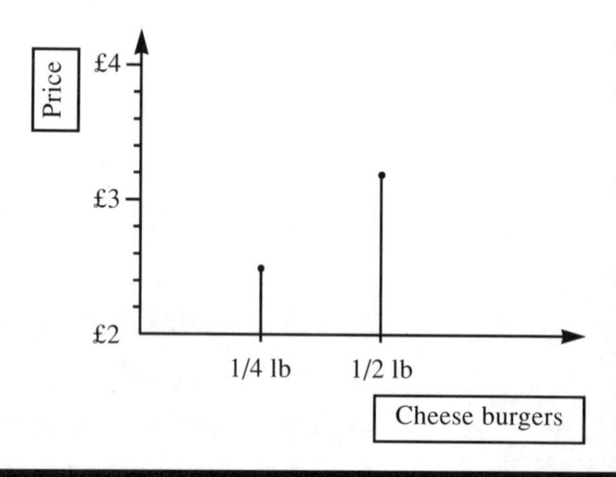

Interpreting the data – sample questions

- How many different burgers are there altogether?
- Which burgers cost £2.45, £3.15, ...?
- Which burgers are the same price?
- How many different choices of burger can be made with £3?
- How much more for a 1/4 lb chilli burger than a 1/4 lb diet burger?
- How much extra for ordering a 1/2 lb instead of a 1/4 lb for yankee, salad, ...?
- How much change from £3 for each 1/4 lb burger?
- How much change from £5 for each 1/2 lb burger?

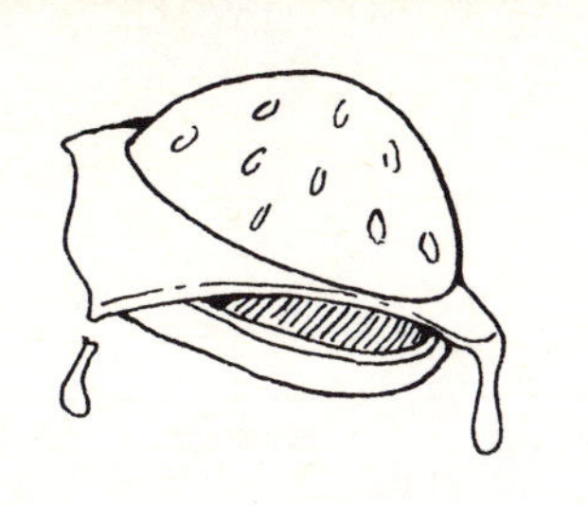

Burgers

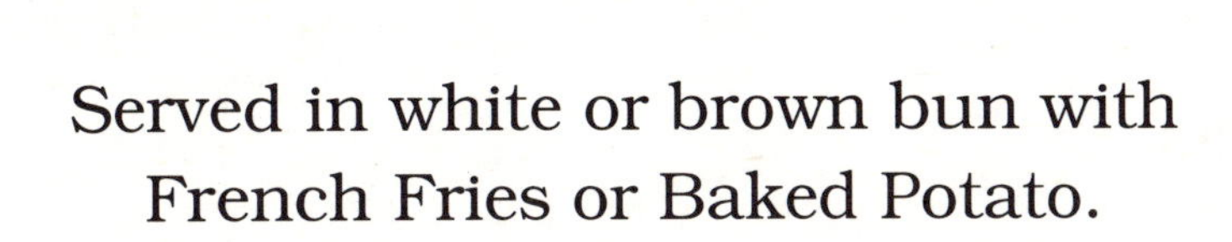

Served in white or brown bun with
French Fries or Baked Potato.

1/4 lb		1/2 lb
£2.15	YANKEE BURGER (straight)	£2.90
£2.30	DIET BURGER (salad in place of chips and bun)	£2.99
£2.45	CHILLI BURGER (topped with cheese)	£3.15
£2.50	CHEESE BURGER (topped with cheese)	£3.20
£2.50	SALAD BURGER (with lettuce, tomato and cucumber)	£3.20
£2.80	SUPER BURGER (with bacon and melted cheese)	£3.60

9 Birthdays

Frequency tables

Bar graphs

Data collection

Constructing a frequency table for the day of the week for each pupil's birthday this year. Drawing a bar graph to represent the data.

LEVEL	Profile Component 1				Profile Component 2		
	UA	N	A	M	UA	S	D
1							
2					●		●
3					●		●
4					●		
5							
6							
7							
8							
9							
10							

D2 Frequency table.
D3 Bar graph.

Activity

Use this year's calendar to find the day of the week for each pupil's birthday. Provide either a list of the pupil's birth dates, or a list of the days on which their birthdays fall.

Handling the data – sample activities

- Complete the frequency table on the sheet (**collect, process data**), then draw a bar graph to illustrate the results (**represent data**). Colour or shade the bar graph. Write about it (**interpret data**).
- **Collect data** from another class, draw a graph and compare the two. Write about them (**using and applying; process, record, represent, interpret data**).

Interpreting the data – sample questions

- How many birthdays fall on Wednesdays?
- How many birthdays fall at weekends, weekdays?
- Which day of the week has the most/fewest birthdays?
- How many more birthdays fall on Monday than Friday?
- How many fewer birthdays fall on Thursday than Sunday?
- Which days have more than five birthdays, less than four birthdays, ...?
- How many other children have a birthday on the same day as you?

Birthdays

Birthday		Total
Monday		
Tuesday		
Wednesday		
Thursday		
Friday		
Saturday		
Sunday		

Day of birthdays

Children

7
6
5
4
3
2
1

Monday Tuesday Wednesday Thursday Friday Saturday Sunday

more
DATA HANDLING
SPECTRUM MATHS

10 Sponsored walk

Block graphs

Bar graphs

Bar line graphs

Tables

Interpreting a table showing the number of miles walked by each of a group of children together with their amounts of sponsorship. Drawing block graphs, bar graphs and bar line graphs to illustrate the data.

LEVEL	Profile Component 1				Profile Component 2		
	UA	N	A	M	UA	S	D
1							
2							●
3		●					●
4							●
5							
6							
7							
8							
9							
10							

N3 Money problems.
D2 Block graphs.
D3 Tables. Bar graphs.
D4 Bar line graphs.

Handling the data – sample activities

- Draw a block graph to show the number of miles each walked (**represent data**).
- Draw a bar graph to show the amount each walker was sponsored for (**represent data**).
- Calculate how much each walker collected (**process data**).
- Draw a graph to show how much each walker earned (**represent data**).

Interpreting the data – sample questions

- How many miles did Evan, Kofi, walk?
- Who walked 5 miles, 4 miles, ...?
- Who walked the furthest?
- How much further did: Lynn walk than Damian, Kofi walk than Anna, ...?
- How much was Karen sponsored for?
- Who was sponsored for 12p per mile, 6p per mile, ...?
- How much did Evan, Lynn, ... earn?

Sponsored walk

Name	Distance walked in miles	Sponsorship per mile
Evan	5	10p
Karen	3	8p
Lynn	6	5p
Damian	2	15p
Anna	4	12p
Kofi	6	6p

Write some sentences about this table.

11 Five colours

Frequency tables

Bar graphs

Throwing a dice whose faces are coloured differently. (Two are the same, the rest are different.) Completing a frequency table and drawing a bar graph to show the results.

LEVEL	Profile Component 1				Profile Component 2		
	UA	N	A	M	UA	S	D
1							
2					●		●
3					●		●
4					●		
5							
6							
7							
8							
9							
10							

D2 Frequency table.
D3 Bar graph.

Apparatus

Make a dice by colouring the faces of a cube: two red, one blue, one yellow, one green and one white.

Activity

Throw the dice 20 times and record the colour of the showing face in the table provided.

Handling the data – sample activities

- Complete the frequency table (**collect process data**), then draw a bar graph to illustrate the results of the experiment (**represent data**). Write some sentences about the graph (**interpret data**).
- Repeat the experiment and compare the results with the first experiment (**using and applying**).
- Devise different experiments by colouring the faces of cubes in different ways (**using and applying**).

Interpreting the data – sample questions

- How many of the throws showed red, blue, ...?
- Which colours appeared three times, two times, four times, ...?
- Which colour appeared most often, next most often, ...?
- How many more times did red show than green, ...?
- How many fewer times did white show than blue, ...?
- How many of the throws showed yellow or green, ...?
- How many of the throws were not red?
- Do you think the same thing would happen if the experiment were repeated?

Five colours

11

Make a dice by colouring the faces of a cube: two red, one blue, one yellow, one green and one white.

Colour		Total
RED		
BLUE		
YELLOW		
GREEN		
WHITE		

12 Addition tables

Tables

Bar graphs

Constructing and analysing the results of addition tables.
Drawing block graphs to illustrate the distribution of the sums.

Activity

Complete the two addition tables on the sheet.

LEVEL	Profile Component 1				Profile Component 2		
	UA	N	A	M	UA	S	D
1							
2		●	●		●		●
3		●	●		●		●
4					●		
5							
6							
7							
8							
9							
10							

N2/N3 Addition facts.
A2/A3 Number patterns.
D2 Block graphs.
D3 Tables.

Handling the data – sample activities

- Draw graphs to show the frequency of occurrence of the sums in each addition table (**represent data**).
- Invent your own addition tables, then draw graphs to illustrate the outcomes. Write some sentences about the results (**using and applying; process, represent, interpret data).**

Interpreting the data – sample questions

- What is 3 + 4, 2 + 5, 4 + 4, ...?
- Which additions give a total of 8, ...?
- Which totals occurred three times, two times, ...?
- Which totals occurred the same number of times?
- How many different totals are there altogether?
- Which total occurred most often, least often?
- How many more totals of 6 than totals of 4, ...?

Addition tables

+	1	2	3	4	5
1	2	3	4	5	6
2	3	4	5	6	7
3	4	5	6	7	8
4	5	6	7	8	9
5	6	7	8	9	10

Totals from the addition table

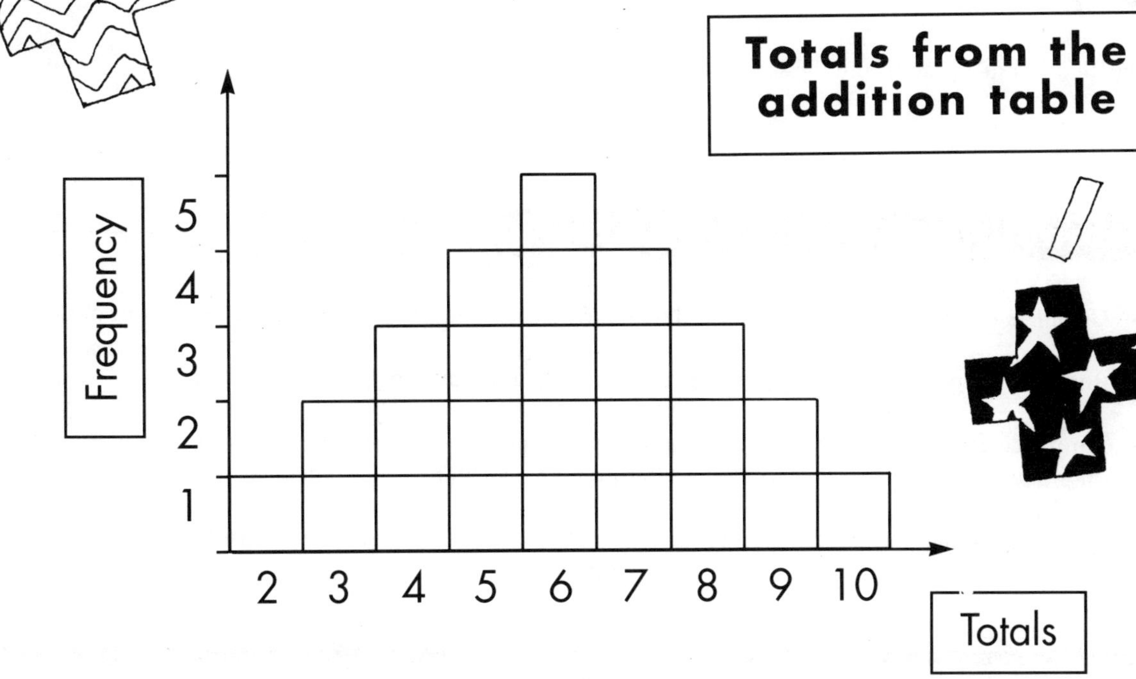

+	3	4	5	6	7
3					
4					
5					
6					
7					

+	1	3	5	7	9
0					
1					
2					
3					
4					

13 Dice scores

Frequency tables

Bar graphs

Data collection

Constructing a frequency table based on the throws of a dice.
Drawing a bar graph to illustrate the results.

LEVEL	Profile Component 1				Profile Component 2		
	UA	N	A	M	UA	S	D
1							
2					●		●
3					●		●
4					●		
5							
6							
7							
8							
9							
10							

D2 Frequency table.
D3 Bar graph.

Apparatus

Use one dice numbered 1 to 6.

Activity

Throw the dice 36 times, and record the score in the frequency table on the sheet.

Handling the data – sample activities

- Complete the frequency table (**process data**), then draw a bar graph of the results (**represent data**).
- Repeat the experiment and compare the results (**using and applying**).
- Throw the dice but add 3 to the **dice number** for the score. Do this 36 times, record the results and draw a graph to illustrate them (**using and applying; record, process, represent data).**
- Try the experiment with a dice numbered differently, e.g. 3, 4, 5, 6, 7, 8, (**using and applying**).

Interpreting the data – sample questions

- How many throws scored 1, scored 2, ...?
- Which score occurred most often, least often?
- Which scores occurred more than 6, fewer than 6, ... times?
- How many more 2s than 5s?
- How many fewer 3s than 4s?
- How many throws scored more than 4, fewer than 3?
- If you repeated the experiment, which score do you think will occur most often?
- Can you guess how many 4s there will be from 24 throws?

Dice scores

You will need
one dice numbered
1 to 6.

Throw the dice 36 times. Record the score for each throw.

Score		Total
1		
2		
3		
4		
5		
6		

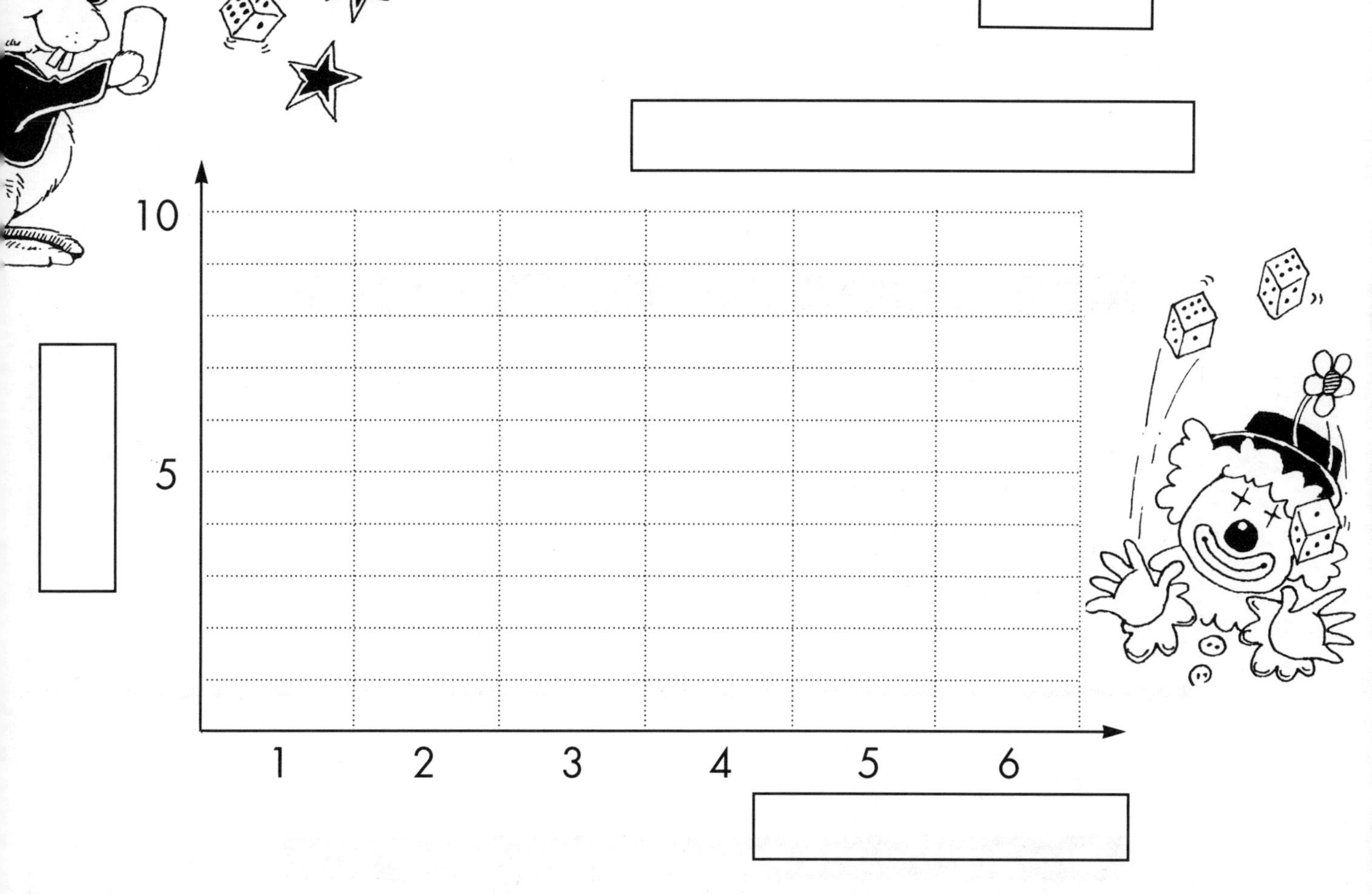

Score		Total
1	~~||||~~ ||	7
2	~~||||~~	5
3	~~||||~~ ||||	9
4	~~||||~~	5
5	||||	4
6	~~||||~~ |	6
		36

Scores on a dice

Total

10
5

1 2 3 4 5 6

Score

more
DATA HANDLING
SPECTRUM MATHS

14 Papers

Pictograms

Data collection

Interpreting and drawing a pictogram relating to the family newspaper. Collecting data on family newspapers and illustrating the results with a pictogram.

LEVEL	Profile Component 1				Profile Component 2		
	UA	N	A	M	UA	S	D
1							
2					●		
3					●		●
4					●		
5							
6							
7							
8							
9							
10							

D3 Pictograms.

Handling the data – sample activities

- **Collect data** for family newspapers for your class and draw a pictogram (**represent data**). Write about it (**interpret data**).
- **Collect data** from another class, combine it with yours, draw a pictogram and write about it (**using and applying; process, record, represent, interpret data**).
- **Collect data** about family newspapers for the teachers and staff in the school and draw a graph (**using and applying**).

Interpreting the data – sample questions

- How many families read the *Sun*, *Express*, ...?
- Which paper is read by five families, two families, ...?
- Which is the most popular, least popular newspaper?
- How many more families read the *Mail* than the *Sun*?
- How many families read the *Mirror* or the *Mail*?
- How many families altogether?
- Which newspapers are read by more than four families?
- Which newspapers are read by fewer than four families?

Papers

This data shows the newspapers taken by some families.

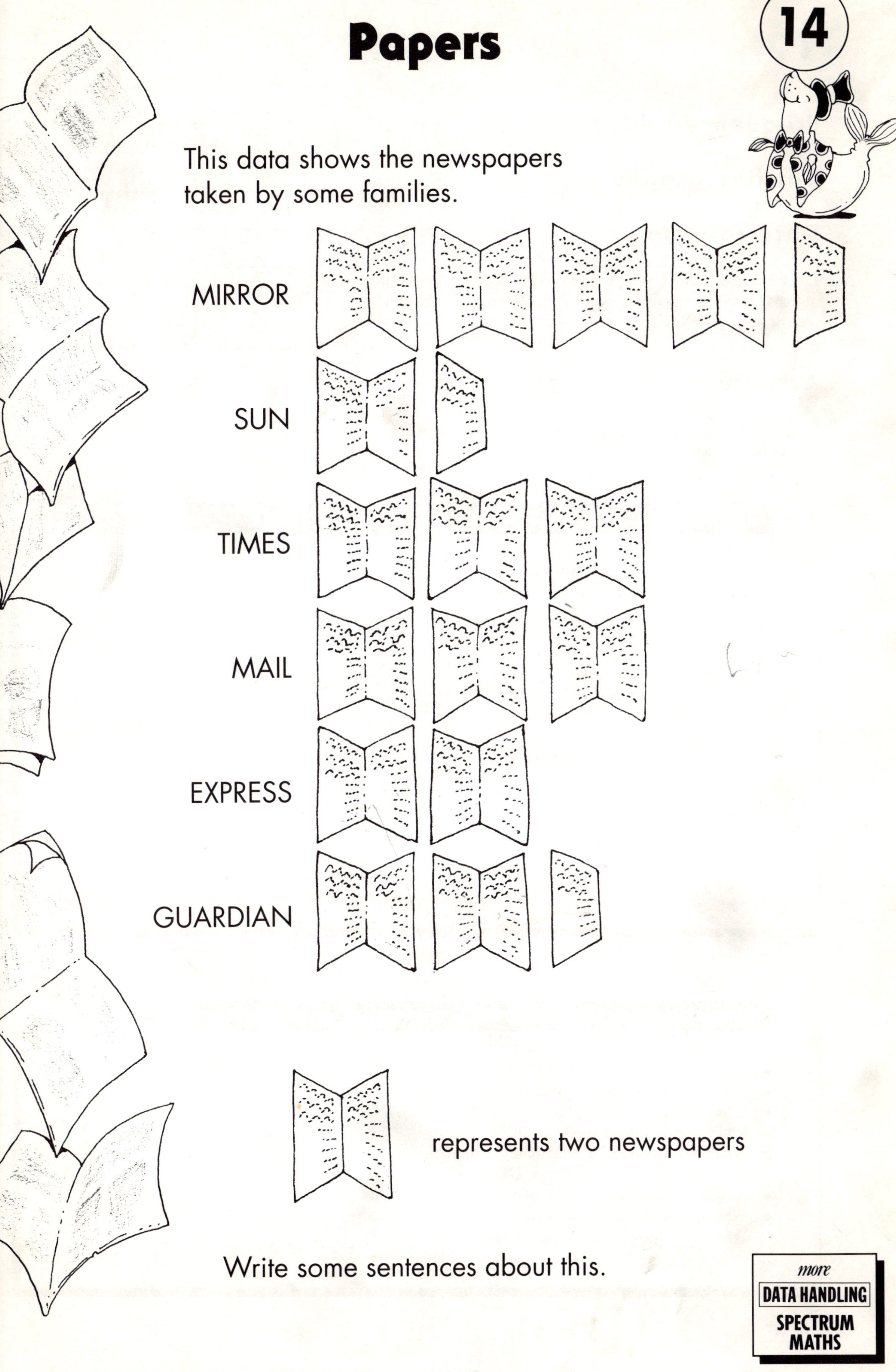

Write some sentences about this.

15 Letter count

Frequency tables

Bar line graphs

Data collection

Constructing a frequency table based on the occurrences of letters of the alphabet from a passage of writing. Interpreting the table, then drawing a bar line graph to illustrate the data.

LEVEL	Profile Component 1				Profile Component 2		
	UA	N	A	M	UA	S	D
1							
2					●		●
3					●		
4					●		●
5							
6							
7							
8							
9							
10							

D2 Frequency tables.
D4 Bar line graphs.

Activity

Read through the passage and construct a tally chart for the occurrence of each letter.

Handling the data – sample activities

- Draw a bar line graph to illustrate the data (**represent data**), and write about it (**interpret data**).
- Choose your own passage of writing and construct a frequency table for the occurrences of letters (**collect, process, record data**). Then draw a graph to illustrate the data (**represent data**). Compare the two graphs (**using and applying; interpret data**).

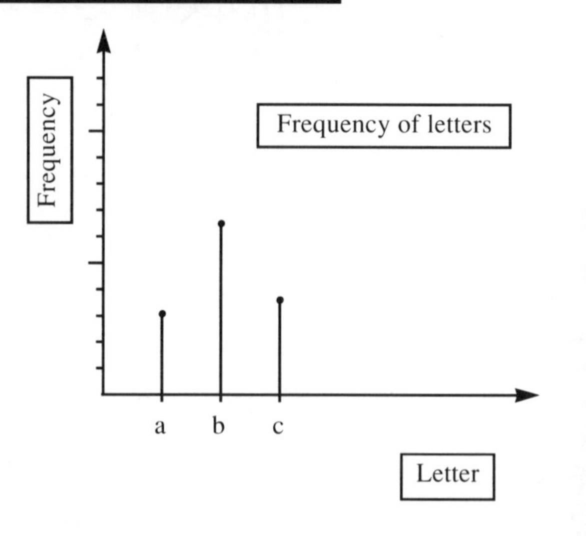

Interpreting the data – sample questions

- How many times did the letter a, d, q, ... appear?
- Which letter appeared ___ times?
- Which letter was the most frequent, least frequent, ...?
- Which letters did not appear at all?
- Which letters appeared more than ___ times?
- Which letters appeared only once?
- How many times did the vowels occur?
- Which vowel occurred most often?
- Which consonant occurred most often?

Letter count

Mr Wonka was standing all alone just inside the open gates of the factory.
And what an extraordinary little man he was!
He had a black top hat on his head.
He wore a tail coat made of a beautiful plum-coloured velvet.
His trousers were bottle green.
His gloves were pearly grey.
And in one hand he carried a fine gold-topped walking cane.

From *Charlie and the Chocolate Factory* by Roald Dahl (Unwin Hyman)

Letter	Tally	Total
a		
b		
c		
d		
e		
f		
g		
h		
i		
j		
k		
l		
m		
n		

Letter	Tally	Total
o		
p		
q		
r		
s		
t		
u		
v		
w		
x		
y		
z		

16 Months

Tables

Reading a calendar month and considering relationships between days, weeks and months.

LEVEL	Profile Component 1				Profile Component 2		
	UA	N	A	M	UA	S	D
1							
2				●			
3							●
4							
5							
6							
7							
8							
9							
10							

M2 Units of time.
D3 Reading lists, tables.

Handling the data – sample activities

- Draw a calendar for the current month and write about it (**interpret data**).
- Compare one month with another (**interpret data**).

Interpreting the data – sample questions

- How many days are there in April?
- What day of the week is the first of the month, last day of the month?
- What day is May 1st?
- What day is March 31st?
- How many Tuesdays are there in April, how many Sundays, ...?
- What date is the second Tuesday, the third Saturday, ...?
- What are the dates of the Saturdays in April?

Months

Mon.	Tues.	Wed.	Thurs.	Fri.	Sat.	Sun.
						1
2	3	4	5	6	7	8
9	10	11	12	13	14	15
16	17	18	19	20	21	22
23	24	25	26	27	28	29
30						

Write some sentences
about this month.

17 Telephone numbers

Frequency tables
Bar graphs
Data collection

Constructing a frequency table to represent the frequency of digit occurrence in a set of ten telephone numbers. Interpreting the table. Drawing a bar graph to represent the data.

LEVEL	Profile Component 1				Profile Component 2		
	UA	N	A	M	UA	S	D
1							
2					●		●
3					●		●
4					●		
5							
6							
7							
8							
9							
10							

D2 Frequency tables.
D3 Bar graphs.

Activity

Construct a frequency table.

Digit		Total
0	////	4
1	///	3
2	~~////~~ ////	9
3	////	4
4	~~////~~ /	6
5	~~////~~ ~~////~~	10
6	~~////~~ ////	9
7	~~////~~ //	7
8	~~////~~	5
9	///	3

Handling the data – sample activities

- Draw a bar graph to show the distribution of the digits (**represent data**).
- **Collect data** from another set of ten telephone numbers from the telephone directory, construct a frequency table for the occurrence of digits, and then draw a graph. Compare the two (**using and applying; record, process, represent, interpret data**).

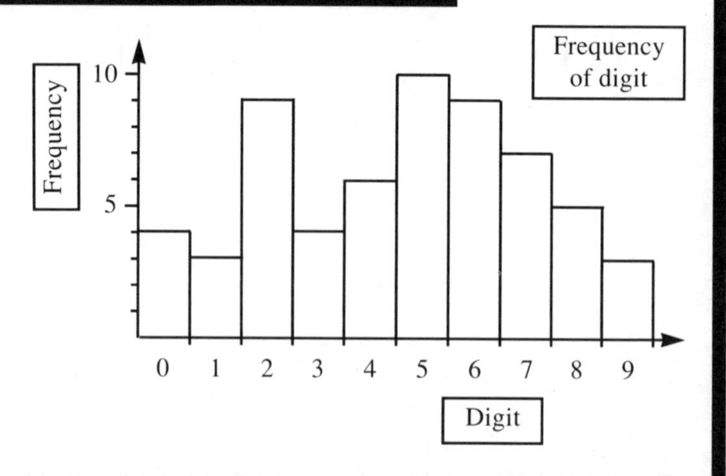

Interpreting the data – sample questions

- How many 4s, 8s, ...?
- Which digit occurs nine times, five times, ...?
- Which digit occurs most often, next most often, ...?
- Which digit occurs least often?
- How many more 7s than 3s are there, ...?
- How many fewer 9s than 2s are there, ...?
- Which digits occur an equal number of times?
- Which digits occur more than eight times, fewer than five times, ...?

Telephone numbers

Howe J.W, 56 Barncliffe Rd		301654
Howe J.W, 29 Ironside Pl		375638
Howe J.W, 18 Laburnam Gro		866385
Howe J.W, 40 Mauncer Cres		692257
Howe K, Hilltop Fm, Dalton Magna		851777
Howe K, 6 Bramley Grange Dv		546248
Howe K, 69 Deerlands Mt		322662
Howe K, 111 Dundas Rd		442558
Howe K, 21 Helmsley Av		476271
Howe K, 38 Liberty Dv		336586
Howe Kenneth, 26 Lime Tree Av		545700
Howe K, 10 Muirfield Av,		580930
Howe K, 85 Tapton Hill Rd		661295
Howe L, 39 Barkers Rd		580213
Howe L, 3 Brushfield Gro		392384
Howe L, 375 Greenland Wy		448247
Howe L, 78 Longley Hall Gro		437103
Howe L, 13 Milnrow Cres		322625

Digit		Total
0		
1		
2		
3		
4		
5		
6		
7		
8		
9		

18 Arsenal v Liverpool

Frequency tables

Bar graphs

Lists

Analysis of data relating to the results of football matches between Arsenal and Liverpool over 20 years. Constuction of frequency table leading to bar graphs.

LEVEL	Profile Component 1				Profile Component 2		
	UA	N	A	M	UA	S	D
1							
2							●
3							●
4							
5							
6							
7							
8							
9							
10							

D2 Frequency tables.
D3 Read lists. Bar graphs.

Handling the data – sample activities

- Consider the Liverpool v Arsenal matches. Analyse the number of games won by Liverpool, Arsenal and drawn. Repeat for the Arsenal v Liverpool matches (**process, interpret data**).
- Draw a frequency table for the results of the matches (**process data**). Draw a graph to illustrate the data (**represent data**).

Result		Total
0 – 0		
1 – 0		
1 – 1		
2 – 0		
2 – 1		
2 – 2		

- Construct a frequency table for the number of goals scored per match. Draw a bar chart to illustrate the data. Write about it (**process, represent, interpret data**).

Interpreting the data – sample questions

Consider the Livepool v Arsenal matches:

- What was the score in 1979–80, 1986–87, ...?
- Who won in 1983–84, 1988–89, ...?
- In which season was the score 2–0, 1–1, ...?
- In which season were five goals scored, four goals scored, ...?
- In which seasons was the result a draw?
- In how many matches did a team score three goals, no goals, ...?

Arsenal v Liverpool

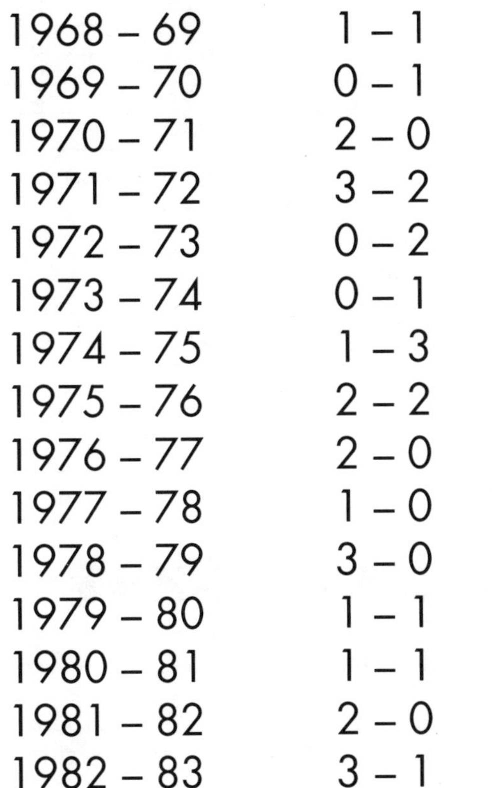

	LIVERPOOL V ARSENAL	ARSENAL v LIVERPOOL
1968 – 69	1 – 1	1 – 1
1969 – 70	0 – 1	2 – 1
1970 – 71	2 – 0	2 – 0
1971 – 72	3 – 2	0 – 0
1972 – 73	0 – 2	0 – 0
1973 – 74	0 – 1	0 – 2
1974 – 75	1 – 3	2 – 0
1975 – 76	2 – 2	1 – 0
1976 – 77	2 – 0	1 – 1
1977 – 78	1 – 0	0 – 0
1978 – 79	3 – 0	1 – 0
1979 – 80	1 – 1	0 – 0
1980 – 81	1 – 1	1 – 0
1981 – 82	2 – 0	1 – 1
1982 – 83	3 – 1	0 – 2
1983 – 84	2 – 1	0 – 2
1984 – 85	3 – 0	3 – 1
1985 – 86	2 – 0	2 – 0
1986 – 87	2 – 1	0 – 1
1987 – 88	2 – 0	1 – 2
1988 – 89	0 – 2	1 – 1

Which team has the best record?

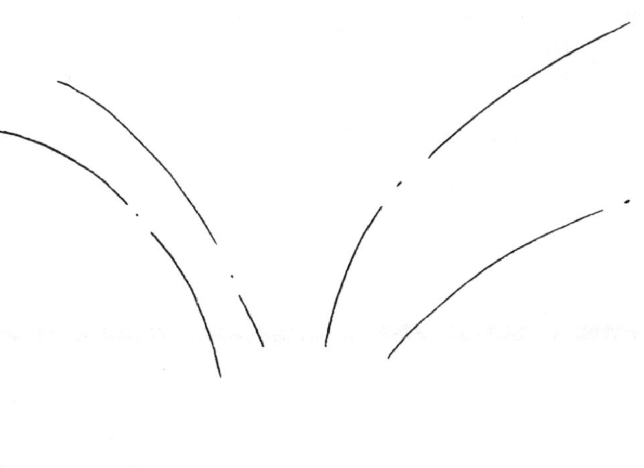

19 Car occupants

Frequency tables

Bar graphs

Data collection

Collecting data based on the number of occupants of cars.
Drawing a frequency table and bar chart.

LEVEL	Profile Component 1				Profile Component 2		
	UA	N	A	M	UA	S	D
1							
2							●
3							●
4							
5							
6							
7							
8							
9							
10							

D2 Frequency tables.
D3 Bar charts.

Activity

Conduct a traffic survey by recording the number of occupants of 25 cars as they pass by. Draw a frequency table and then a bar chart to illustrate the data.

Handling the data – sample activities

- Write some sentences about the bar chart (**interpret data**).
- **Collect data** on another 25 cars, combine this with the previous 25 cars to form a frequency table based on 50 cars (**record, process data**). Draw a graph to illustrate the results (**represent data**).

Interpreting the data – sample questions

- How many cars had no passengers?
- How many cars contained two people, three people, ...?
- What number of occupants is most common?
- How many more cars contained two people than four people?
- How many cars had an odd number, even number of people?
- Of all the 25 cars surveyed did more or fewer than half of them have no passengers?

Car occupants

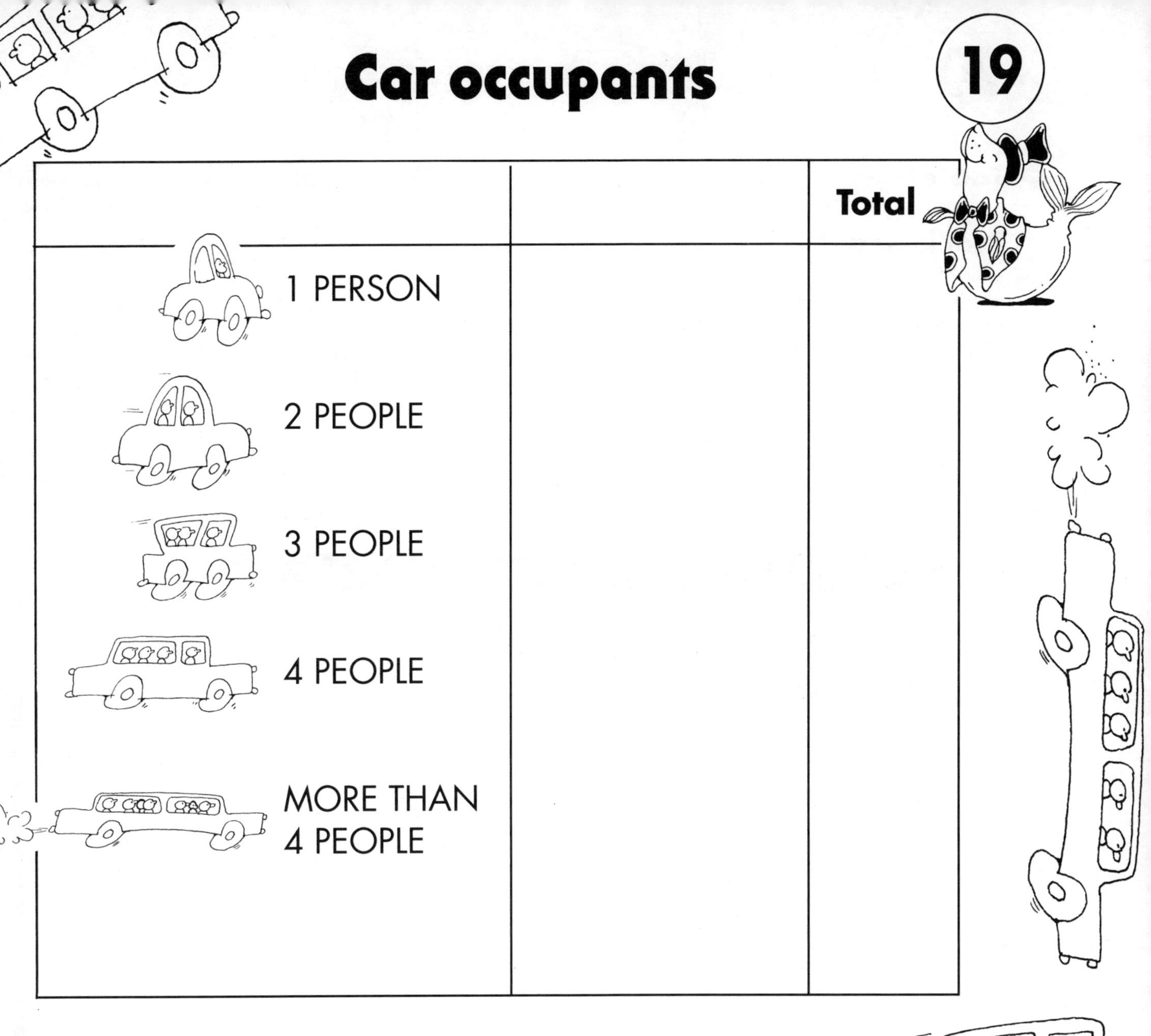

		Total
1 PERSON		
2 PEOPLE		
3 PEOPLE		
4 PEOPLE		
MORE THAN 4 PEOPLE		

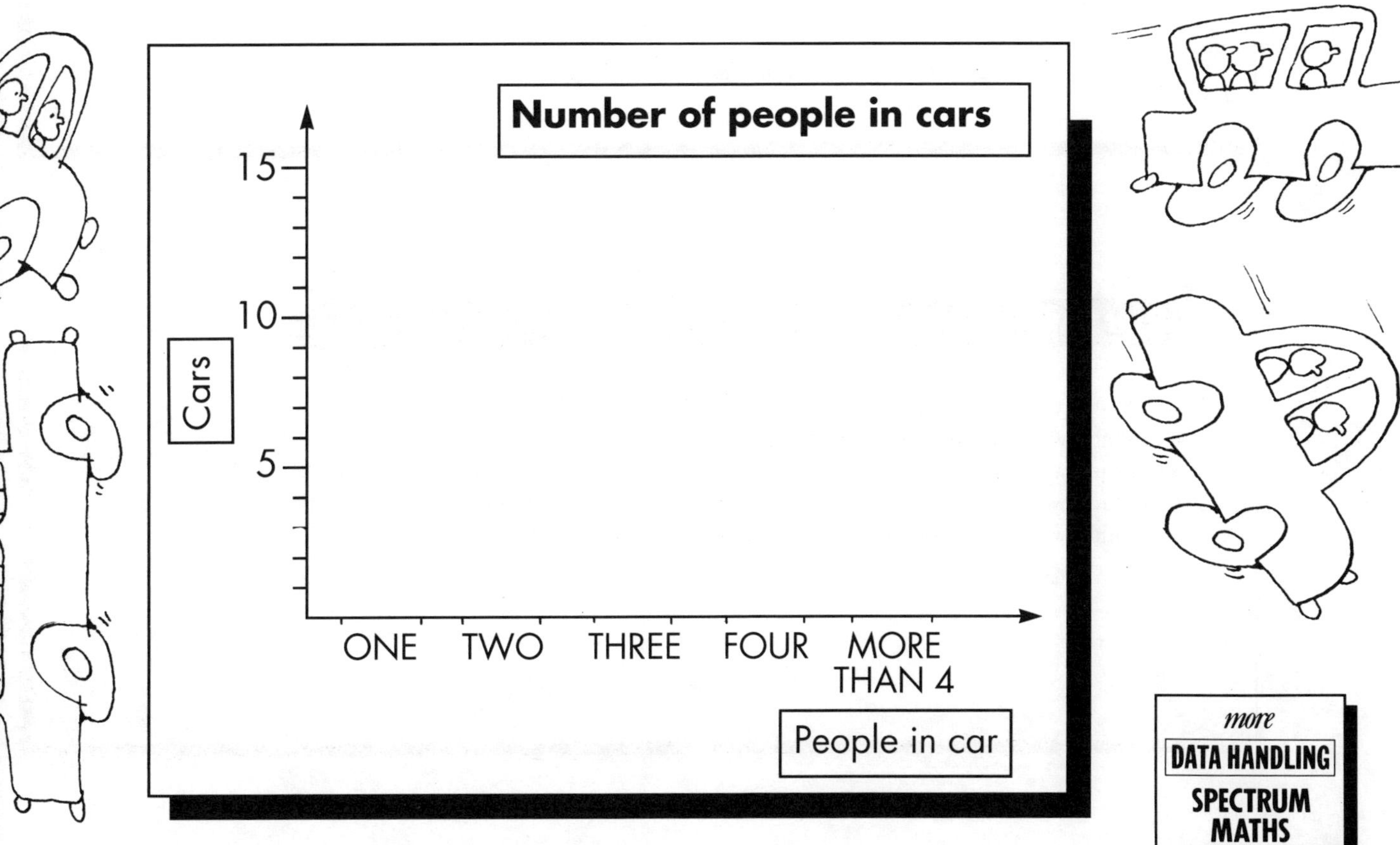

more
DATA HANDLING
SPECTRUM MATHS

Number words

Tables

Block graphs

Interpreting a table and block graph showing the number of letters in the words for numbers from one to ten. Construction of tables and block graphs for other number words.

LEVEL	Profile Component 1				Profile Component 2		
	UA	N	A	M	UA	S	D
1							
2					●		●
3					●		●
4					●		
5							
6							
7							
8							
9							
10							

D2 Block graphs.
D3 Reading tables.

Handling the data – sample activities

- Write some sentences about the block graph (**interpret data**).

6	7	8	9
ELEVEN TWELVE TWENTY	FIFTEEN SIXTEEN	THIRTEEN FOURTEEN EIGHTEEN NINETEEN	SEVENTEEN

- Construct a table showing the number of letters in the words for 11–20 (**collect, process data**). Draw a graph to illustrate the results (**represent data**).

2	3	4	5	6
UN	UNE SIX DIX	DEUX SEPT HUIT NEUF CINQ	TROIS	QUATRE

- Anaylse in the same way the French words for the numbers 1–10 (**using and applying**).
- Repeat for words for numbers in other languages (**using and applying**).

Interpreting the data – sample questions

- How many letters in the word three, nine, ...?
- Which words have five letters, three letters, ...?
- Which words have the same number of letters as the word 'seven'?
- Which words have one letter fewer than the word 'four', one letter more than the word 'five'?
- Which word has as many letters as the number it spells?

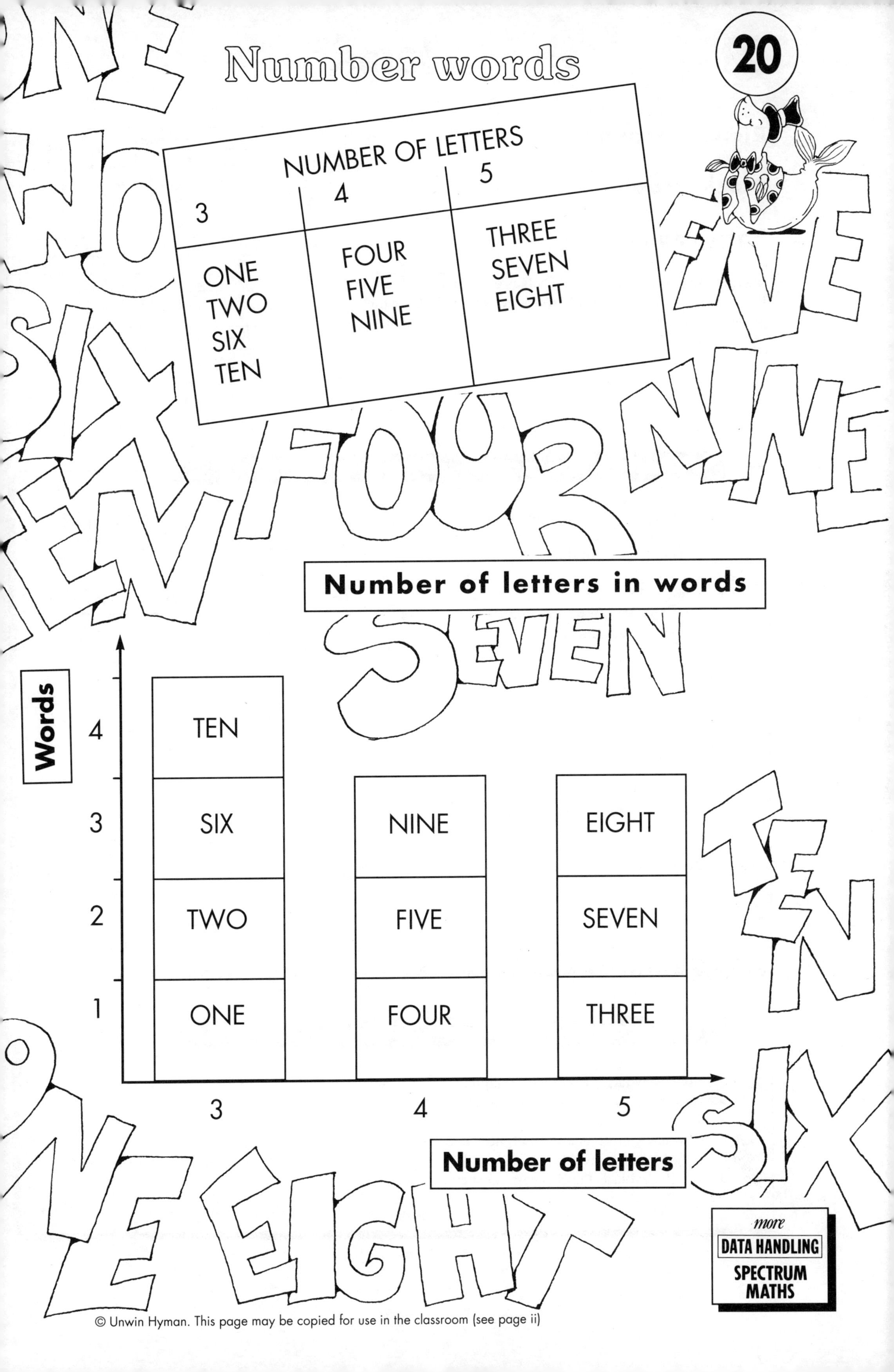

Number words

NUMBER OF LETTERS		
3	4	5
ONE TWO SIX TEN	FOUR FIVE NINE	THREE SEVEN EIGHT

21 Jams

Picture graphs

Block graphs

Bar graphs

Interpreting a picture of the jam shelves of a shop. There are four flavours of jam in two sizes of jars, large and small. Drawing picture graphs, block graphs and bar graphs to illustrate the data.

LEVEL	Profile Component 1				Profile Component 2		
	UA	N	A	M	UA	S	D
1							●
2				●			●
3							●
4							
5							
6							
7							
8							
9							
10							

M2 Comparing sums of money.
D1 Picture graph.
D2 Block graph.
D3 Bar graph.

Handling the data – sample activities

- Draw a picture graph to show the numbers of large and small jars for each flavour (**represent data**).
- Draw a block graph for the number of large jars. Repeat for the number of small jars (**represent data**).
- Draw a bar graph to show the prices of small jars. Repeat for the prices of large jars (**represent data**).

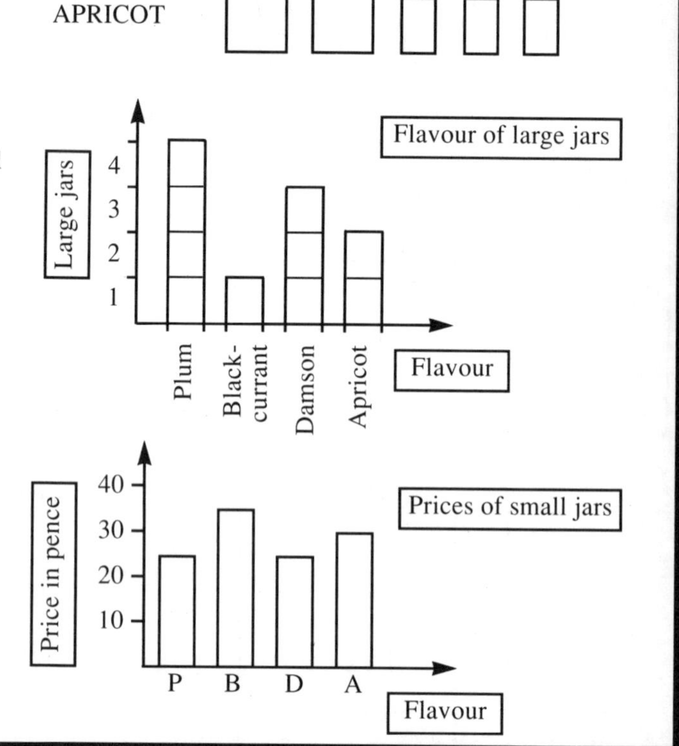

Interpreting the data – sample questions

- How many large jars of damson, plum, ... are there?
- How many small jars of blackcurrant, ... are there?
- Which flavour has the most large jars, most small jars, ..?
- How many more small jars of plum than damson are there?
- If the large jars are 1 kg and the small jars are 1/2 kg, how much plum, apricot, ... altogether?
- Which flavour is the cheapest, most expensive,...?

Jams

PRICES

	LARGE	SMALL
PLUM	50p	25p
BLACKCURRANT	60p	35p
DAMSON	40p	25p
APRICOT	55p	30p

22 Roasts

Tables

Mapping diagrams

Block graphs

Data collection

Interpreting a table showing a group of children's likes of roast dinner. Drawing a similar table for pupils in the class. Drawing a block graph and mapping diagram to illustrate the results.

LEVEL	Profile Component 1				Profile Component 2		
	UA	N	A	M	UA	S	D
1							●
2							●
3							●
4							
5							
6							
7							
8							
9							
10							

D1 Mapping diagrams.
D2 Block graphs.
D3 Reading tables.

Handling the data – sample activities

- **Collect data**, in groups, for favourite roasts and draw a table to show the results (**process data**). Then write some sentences about the table (**interpret data**).
- Draw a block graph/bar graph to show the favourite roasts (**represent data**).
- Draw a mapping diagram to show favourite roasts (**represent data**).

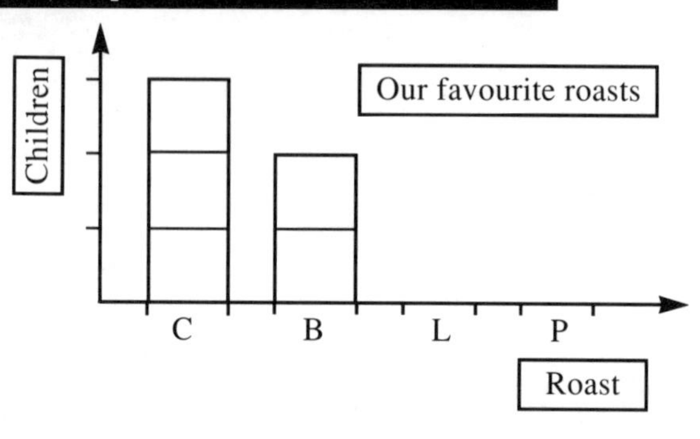

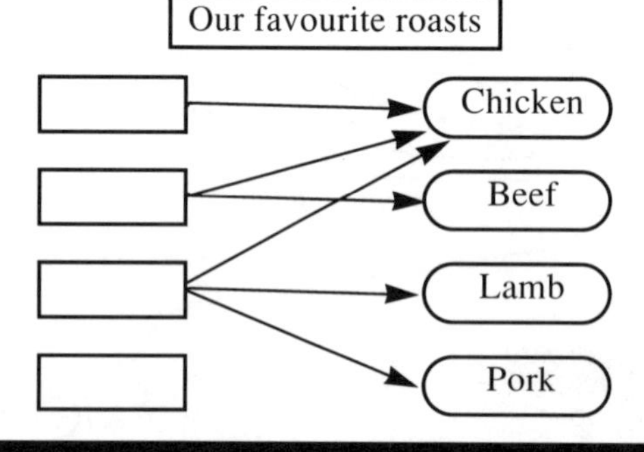

Interpreting the data – sample questions

- What roasts do Pascal, Vanessa, ... like?
- What does Ann, Zoe, ... not like?
- Who likes roast lamb, roast beef, ...?
- How many children like roast chicken, ...?
- How many children do not like roast chicken, ...?
- Who likes everything, nothing, ...?
- Who likes three out of four of the roasts, ...?
- Which is the most popular roast?
- How many more children like roast chicken than roast pork, ...?

Roasts

Roast dinners I like

	Roast chicken	Roast beef	Roast lamb	Roast pork
Pascal		✔		
Ann			✔	
Josie	✔	✔	✔	✔
Zoe	✔			✔
Vanessa			✔	✔
Ben				
Ranjit	✔			

Write sentences about this.

23 News

Bar line graphs

Data collection

Drawing bar line graphs to compare the prices and the number of pages of a set of newspapers. The collection of data from current newspapers and the construction of bar line graphs.

LEVEL	Profile Component 1				Profile Component 2		
	UA	N	A	M	UA	S	D
1							
2		●			●		
3					●		
4					●		●
5							
6							
7							
8							
9							
10							

N2 Number problems involving money.
D4 Bar line graphs.

Handling the data – sample activities

- Draw a bar line graph to show the prices of each paper (**represent data**).
- Draw a bar line graph to show the number of pages for each paper (**represent data**).
- Collect some newspapers, record the data on price and number of pages and draw the corresponding bar line graphs (**using and applying; collect, record, represent data**).

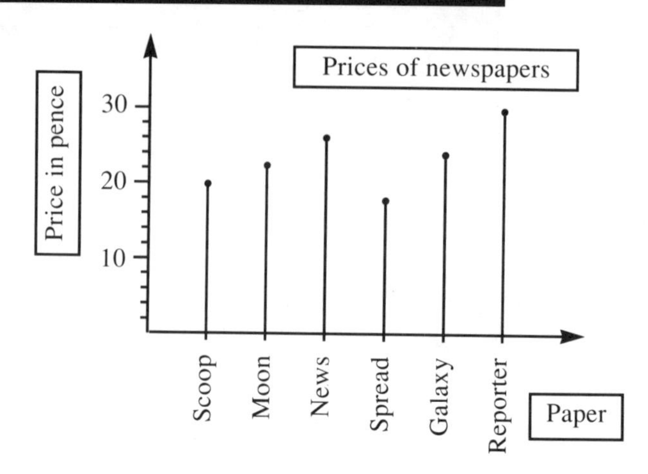

- Repeat for comics instead of newspapers (**using and applying**).

Interpreting the data – sample questions

- How much does the *Galaxy*, *Daily Moon*, ... cost?
- Which paper costs 18p, 26p, ...?
- Which paper costs the most, next most, least, ...?
- How much more does the *Daily News* cost than the *Scoop*, ...?
- How much would it cost to buy the *Scoop* and the *Daily Moon*?
- How many pages in the *News Spread*, *Reporter*, ...?
- Which paper has the most pages, least pages,...?
- Why are the numbers of pages always even numbers?
- Which paper costs 1p per page, more than 1p per page, less than 1p per page?
- How much change from 50p for a *News Spread*, ...?

News

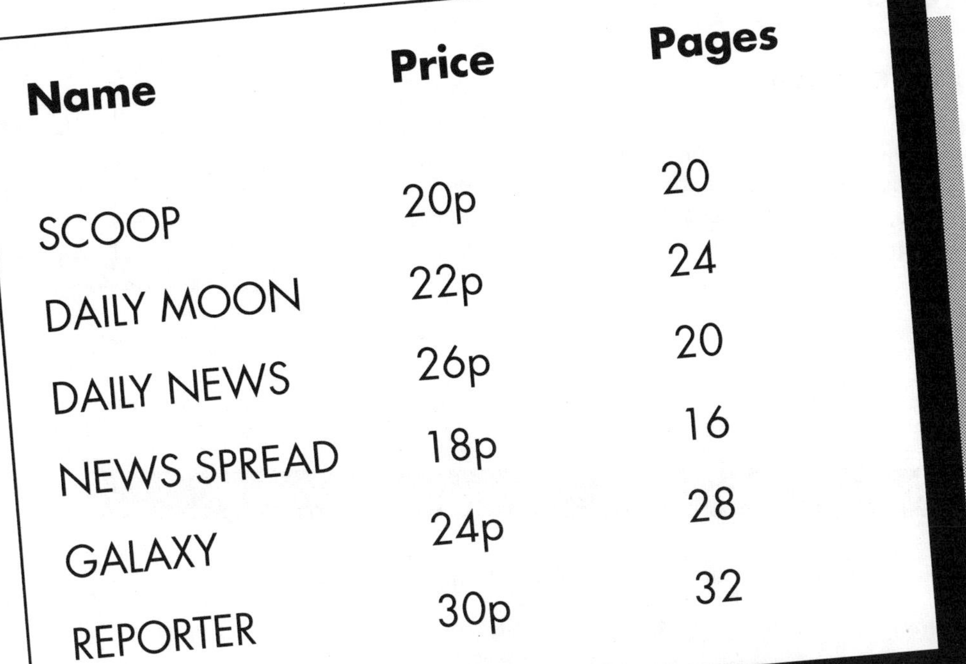

Name	Price	Pages
SCOOP	20p	20
DAILY MOON	22p	24
DAILY NEWS	26p	20
NEWS SPREAD	18p	16
GALAXY	24p	28
REPORTER	30p	32

more
DATA HANDLING
SPECTRUM MATHS

24 Daily use

Tables

Bar charts

Data collection

Comparison of three families in terms of daily food consumption. Constructing a table to make comparisons easier. Collection of data based on pupils own families leading to construction of similar tables. Drawing bar charts to illustrate the data in the tables.

LEVEL	Profile Component 1				Profile Component 2		
	UA	N	A	M	UA	S	D
1							
2					●		
3					●		●
4					●		
5							
6							
7							
8							
9							
10							

D3 Tables. Bar charts.

Handling the data – sample activities

- Draw a table to show the data in simpler form (**process data**). e.g.

Family	Adults	Children	Slices of bread	Bottles of milk	Eggs
Karim	2	2	11	2	4
Bradley	2	3	16	$1\frac{1}{2}$	6
Cohen	2	1	8	3	5

- Draw graphs to show:
  (a) slices of bread eaten per family,
  (b) bottles of milk drunk per family,
  (c) eggs eaten per family, (**represent data**).
- Pupils **collect data** on bread, milk and eggs consumed per day by their family. Construct tables of the data from groups of pupils and analyse them (**using and applying**).

Interpreting the data – sample questions

- Which family is the largest, smallest?
- How many slices of bread and eggs are eaten each day by the Karim family?
- Which family eats the most bread, drinks the most milk, eats the most eggs per day?
- How many more eggs per day do the Bradleys eat than the Cohens?
- How many eggs/slices of bread are eaten per day by all three families together?
- How many slices of bread and eggs do you eat per day?

Daily use

	Bread	Milk	Eggs
Karim Family	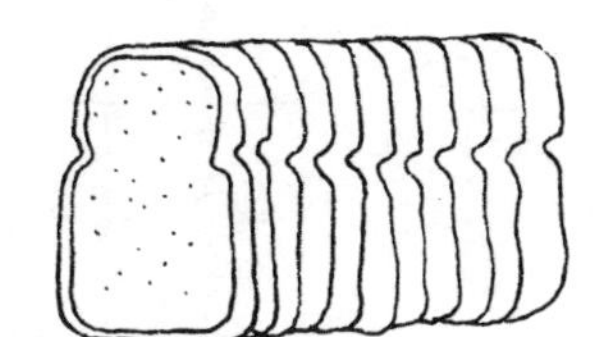		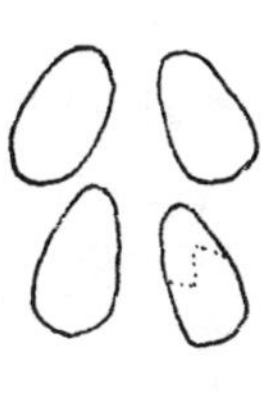
Bradley Family	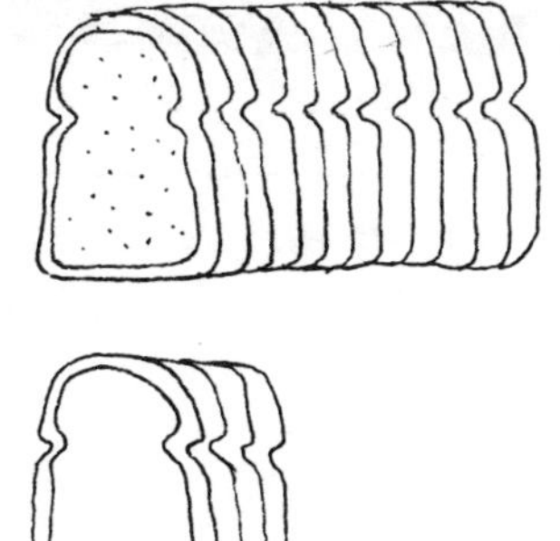		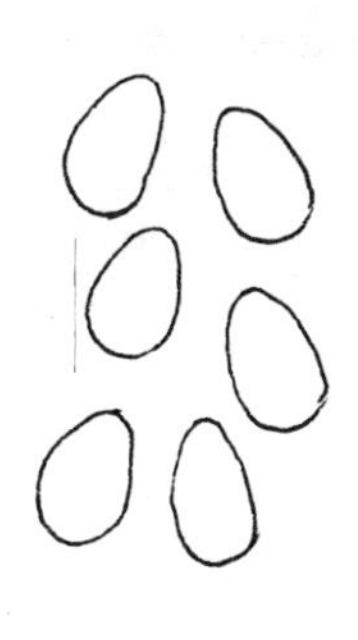
Cohen Family	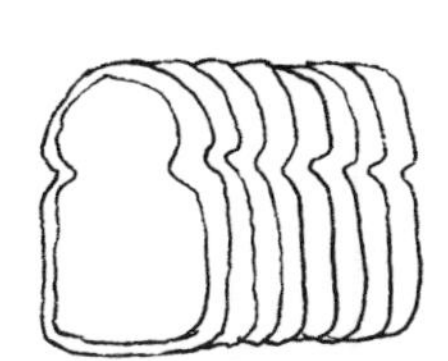	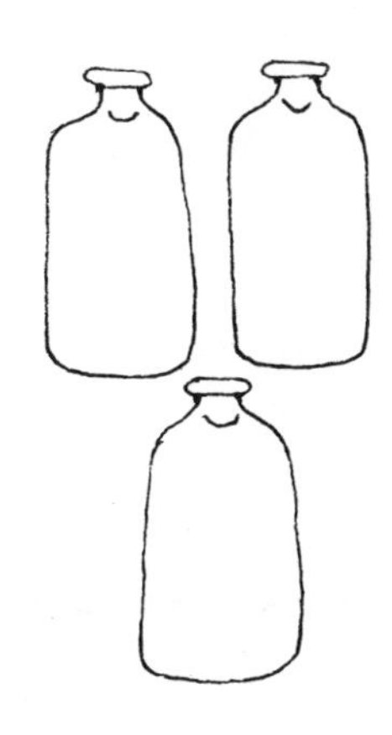	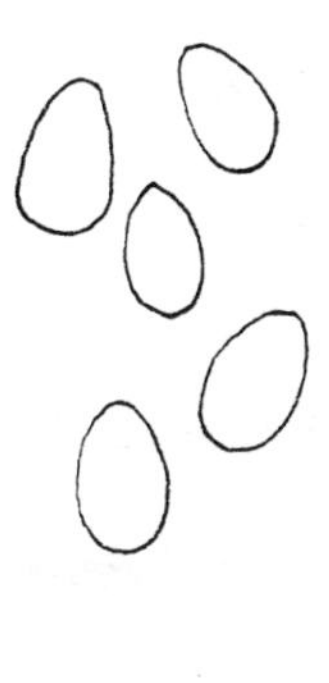

Write some sentences about this.

more
DATA HANDLING
SPECTRUM MATHS

Names

Frequency tables

Bar line graphs

Data collection

Constructing a frequency table to show the occurrence of vowels in a set of first names. Drawing a bar line graph to illustrate the distribution. Collection and analysis of data based on the first names of pupils in class.

LEVEL	Profile Component 1				Profile Component 2		
	UA	N	A	M	UA	S	D
1							
2					●		●
3					●		
4					●		●
5							
6							
7							
8							
9							
10							

D2 Frequency tables.
D4 Bar line graphs.

Handling the data – sample activities

- Construct a frequency table to show the occurrence of the vowels in these first names (**process data**).
- Draw a graph to show the distribution of the vowels (**represent data**).
- Write down the first names of pupils in the class, construct a frequency table, then draw a graph. Write some sentences about the graph (**using and applying; collect, process, represent, interpret data**).
- Collect the names of pupils in another class, analyse the data and compare (**using and applying**).

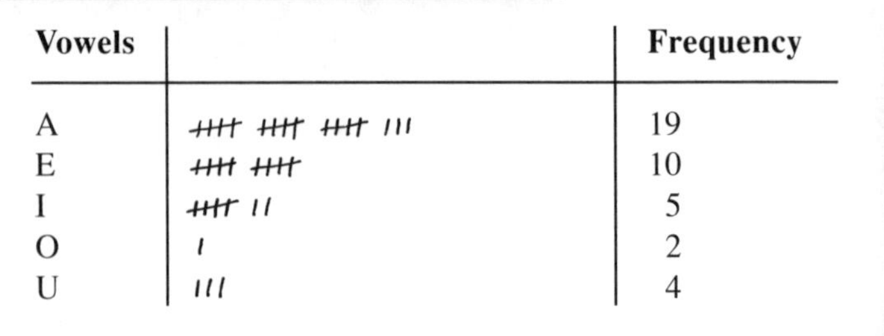

Vowels		Frequency
A	𝍸 𝍸 𝍸 |||	19
E	𝍸 𝍸	10
I	𝍸 ||	5
O			2
U	|||	4

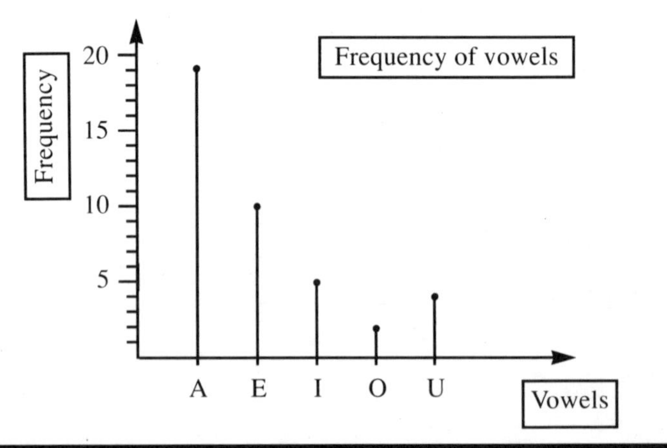

Interpreting the data – sample questions

- Which letters are vowels?
- Which vowels are in the names Hari, Sean, Melanie, ...?
- Which names contain the vowel **i**, ...?
- Which names have two **a**s, **e**s, ...?
- Which names have only one vowel, two vowels, more than two vowels?
- Which name has the most vowels?
- Which names have two non-vowels (consonants)?
- Which names have two different vowels?

Names

GARY
TRACEY
KIRSTY
BALARAMA
MELANIE
NATHAN
TERRY
SEAN
DEREK
LULU

DEAN
PUSHPA
SALLY
ELIZABETH
NICOLA
MANDY
HARI
KELLY
DONNA
SUSAN

How many vowels in each of these names?

more DATA HANDLING SPECTRUM MATHS

26 My friends

Tables

Data collection

Condensing a set of data in tabular form. Collection of data from pupils in the class and tabulating it in different ways.

LEVEL	Profile Component 1				Profile Component 2		
	UA	N	A	M	UA	S	D
1							
2					●		
3					●		●
4					●		
5							
6							
7							
8							
9							
10							

D3 Tables.

Handling the data – sample activities

- Construct tables to condense the data (**process data**). Examples include:

	Blonde	Brown	Black
Boys		Evan Tom	Daljit Nasri
Girls	Ann Hannah	Kate	Meera

	Wears glasses	Doesn't wear glasses
Boy	Evan Nasri	Daljit Tom
Girl	Kate Hannah	Ann Meera

	Blonde hair	Brown hair	Black hair
Wears glasses	Hannah	Evan Kate	Nasri
Doesn't wear glasses	Ann	Tom	Daljit Meera

- **Collect data** on hair colour and the wearing of glasses for pupils in the class and construct some tables to illustrate the results (**using and applying; process, record, represent data**).

Interpreting the data – sample questions

- What colour hair does Evan, Tom, ... have?
- Who wears glasses?
- Who doesn't wear glasses?
- Who has black hair, brown hair, blonde hair?
- Which boys have black hair?
- Which girls wear glasses?
- Which boys do not wear glasses?

My friends

Evan

Ann

Daljit

Evan has brown hair and wears glasses.

Ann does not wear glasses and has blonde hair.

Daljit has black hair and doesn't wear glasses.

Kate wears glasses and has brown hair.

Nasri wears glasses and has black hair.

Meera has black hair and doesn't wear glasses.

Tom does not wear glasses and has brown hair.

Hannah does wear glasses and has blonde hair.

Hannah

Kate

Tom

Meera

Nasri

27 Weighing cubes

Line graphs

Measuring the weight of different numbers of cubes, then drawing a line graph to show the relationship between weight and number of cubes. Interpreting the line graph.

LEVEL	Profile Component 1				Profile Component 2		
	UA	N	A	M	UA	S	D
1							
2					●		
3					●		
4				●	●		●
5							
6							
7							
8							
9							
10							

M4 Measuring weights in grams.
D4 Line graphs.

Activity

Use a pan balance to measure the weights of 20 Unifix cubes, then 40, then 60, 80 and 100.

Handling the data – sample activities

- Record the weights in the table on the sheet (**record data**). Plot the five points, then draw a line graph through the points (**represent data**).
- Weigh 20, 40, 60, 80 and 100 objects other than cubes.
  Examples include: dried peas, conkers, acorns. Record the weights in a table, plot the points on a graph, draw a line graph of best fit, and write some sentences about it (**using and applying; collect, record, represent, interpret data**).

Interpreting the data – sample questions

- How much do 20 cubes weigh?
- How much do 40 cubes weigh? Is this twice as much?
- Use the line graph to estimate the weight of 30 cubes, 70 cubes, ...?
- Use the line graph to estimate how many cubes weigh 100 g, 200 g, ...?
- How much do you think 120 cubes, 200 cubes, ... would weigh?
- How many cubes do you think would weigh 500 g?
- What number of cubes weigh between 110 g and 220 g?

Weighing cubes

27

Number of cubes	Weight in grams
20	
40	
60	
80	
100	

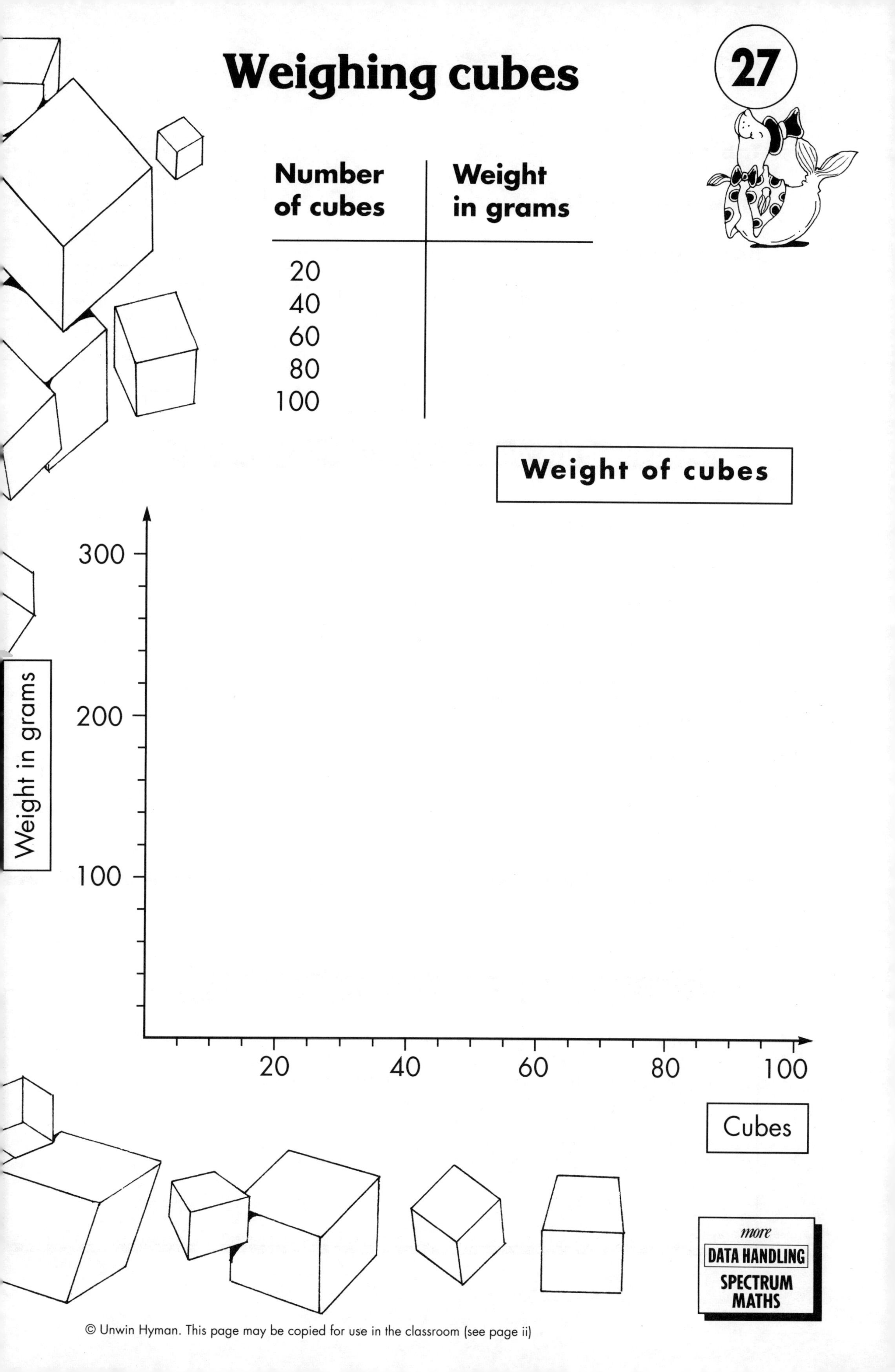

28 Morse code

Tables

Frequency tables

Bar graphs

Construction of a frequency table and drawing a bar graph based on the number of sounds used by the letters in the Morse code.

LEVEL	Profile Component 1				Profile Component 2		
	UA	N	A	M	UA	S	D
1							
2					●		●
3					●		●
4					●		
5							
6							
7							
8							
9							
10							

D2 Frequency tables.
D3 Tables. Bar graphs.

Handling the data – sample activities

- Draw a table to show how many sounds are made by each letter (**process data**).
- Construct a frequency table to show the number of letters which use 1, 2, 3, ... sounds (**process data**). Draw a bar graph to illustrate the table (**represent data**).
- Find some four-sound arrangements of dots and dashes which are not used in the Morse code. How many are there? (**using and applying**).
- How many sounds are needed for the words: one, two, three, ...?

Letter	Sounds
A	2
B	4

Number of sounds		Total
1	//	2
2	////	4
3	~~////~~ ///	8
4	~~////~~ ~~////~~ //	12

- Find some three lettered words which use only four sounds, five sounds, ...

Interpreting the data – sample questions

- What is the Morse code for J, R, ...?
- Which letter is coded —••—, —•, ...?
- How many sounds (dots and dashes) are used for the letter G, Z, ...?
- Which letters use only one sound, two sounds, ...?
- Which letters use dots only, dashes only, ...?
- Are there more dots used than dashes?
- Which letters have two more dots than dashes, dashes than dots, ...?

Morse code

Letter	Code	Letter	Code
A	•–	N	–•
B	–•••	O	–––
C	–•–•	P	•––•
D	–••	Q	––•–
E	•	R	•–•
F	••–•	S	•••
G	––•	T	–
H	••••	U	••–
I	••	V	•••–
J	•–––	W	•––
K	–•–	X	–••–
L	•–••	Y	–•––
M	––	Z	––••

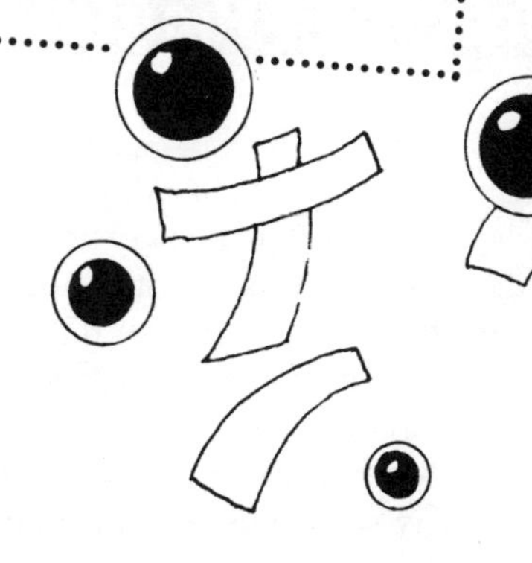

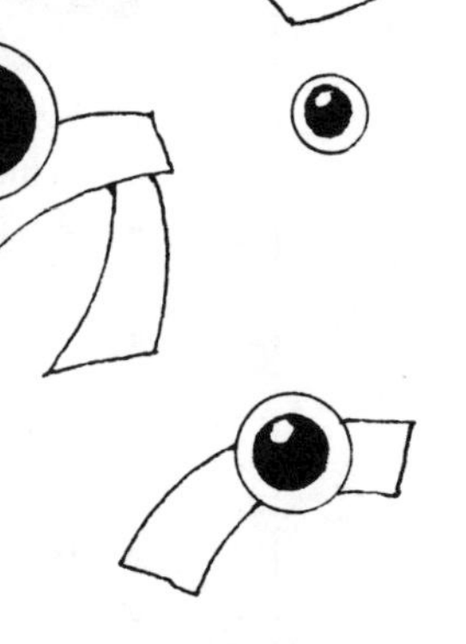

How many sounds are made for each letter?

29 Years

Tables

Reading a year's calendar and considering relationships between days, weeks, months, and years. Prominent dates in the calendar.

LEVEL	Profile Component 1				Profile Component 2		
	UA	N	A	M	UA	S	D
1							
2				●			
3							●
4							
5							
6							
7							
8							
9							
10							

M2 Units of time.
D3 Reading lists, tables.

Handling the data – sample activities

- Choose a month and write some things about it (**interpret data**).
- Colour and label on the calendar some important dates e.g. birthdays, Christmas, school holidays etc. (**process data**).

Interpreting the data – sample questions

- How many days are there in April, September, ...?
- Which months have the most days, fewest days?
- What day of the week is January 1st, February 1st, ...?
- What day of the week is Christmas day, April Fool's day, New Year's Eve, ...?
- What day of the week is your birthday, your brother or sister's birthday, ...?
- How many Sundays are there in June, in July, ...?
- How many days are there in January and February combined?
- How many Saturdays are there in November and December?
- What date/day is the middle of the month of March, of October ...?
- How many Mondays are there in each month?

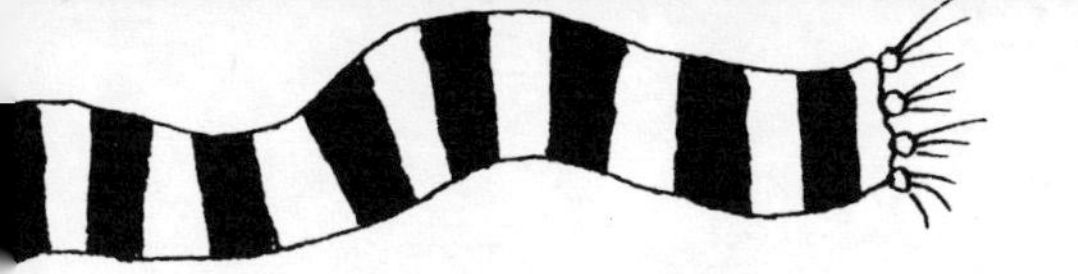

Years

Calendar **1990**

January

M	T	W	T	F	S	S
1	2	3	4	5	6	7
8	9	10	11	12	13	14
15	16	17	18	19	20	21
22	23	24	25	26	27	28
29	30	31				

February

M	T	W	T	F	S	S
			1	2	3	4
5	6	7	8	9	10	11
12	13	14	15	16	17	18
19	20	21	22	23	24	25
26	27	28				

March

M	T	W	T	F	S	S
			1	2	3	4
5	6	7	8	9	10	11
12	13	14	15	16	17	18
19	20	21	22	23	24	25
26	27	28	29	30	31	

April

M	T	W	T	F	S	S
						1
2	3	4	5	6	7	8
9	10	11	12	13	14	15
16	17	18	19	20	21	22
23	24	25	26	27	28	29
30						

May

M	T	W	T	F	S	S
	1	2	3	4	5	6
7	8	9	10	11	12	13
14	15	16	17	18	19	20
21	22	23	24	25	26	27
28	29	30	31			

June

M	T	W	T	F	S	S
				1	2	3
4	5	6	7	8	9	10
11	12	13	14	15	16	17
18	19	20	21	22	23	24
25	26	27	28	29	30	

July

M	T	W	T	F	S	S
						1
2	3	4	5	6	7	8
9	10	11	12	13	14	15
16	17	18	19	20	21	22
23	24	25	26	27	28	29
30	31					

August

M	T	W	T	F	S	S
		1	2	3	4	5
6	7	8	9	10	11	12
13	14	15	16	17	18	19
20	21	22	23	24	25	26
27	28	29	30	31		

September

M	T	W	T	F	S	S
					1	2
3	4	5	6	7	8	9
10	11	12	13	14	15	16
17	18	19	20	21	22	23
24	25	26	27	28	29	30

October

M	T	W	T	F	S	S
1	2	3	4	5	6	7
8	9	10	11	12	13	14
15	16	17	18	19	20	21
22	23	24	25	26	27	28
29	30	31				

November

M	T	W	T	F	S	S
			1	2	3	4
5	6	7	8	9	10	11
12	13	14	15	16	17	18
19	20	21	22	23	24	25
26	27	28	29	30		

December

M	T	W	T	F	S	S
					1	2
3	4	5	6	7	8	9
10	11	12	13	14	15	16
17	18	19	20	21	22	23
24	25	26	27	28	29	30
31						

Write some sentences about this calendar.

30 Twelve shapes

Sorting

Picture graphs

Analysing a set of shapes in terms of their number of sides.
Sorting the shapes.
Names of shapes: triangles, squares, pentagons, ... Constructing picture graphs to illustrate shapes with different numbers of sides.

LEVEL	Profile Component 1				Profile Component 2		
	UA	N	A	M	UA	S	D
1							●
2					●	●	
3					●		
4					●		
5							
6							
7							
8							
9							
10							

S2 Reorganising squares, triangles...
D1 Sorting. Picture graphs.

Handling the data – sample activities

- Write below each shape the number of sides it has (**record data**).
- Cut out the shapes and arrange them according to their number of sides to make a picture graph (**process, represent data**).
- Draw your own set of 12 shapes, cut them out and display them according to their number of sides (**using and applying**).

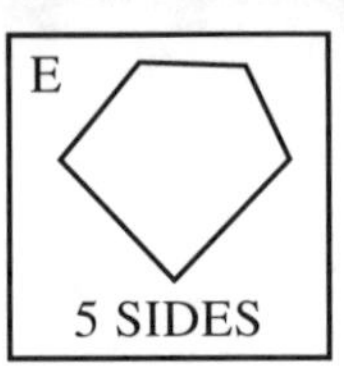

3 SIDES | 4 SIDES | 5 SIDES

A

B

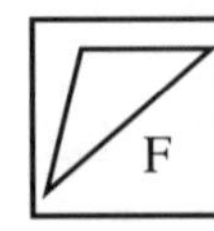

Etc.

Interpreting the data – sample questions

- How many sides does shape D, shape L, ... have?
- Show me a shape with four sides, five sides, ...?
- How many shapes can you find with five sides?
- Which shape has the most number of sides? How many sides does it have?
- Which shapes have more than five sides?
- What name do we give the shapes with three sides?
- What shape is D, L, ...?
- What is the total number of sides for all the shapes in the top row, middle column, ...?

Twelve shapes

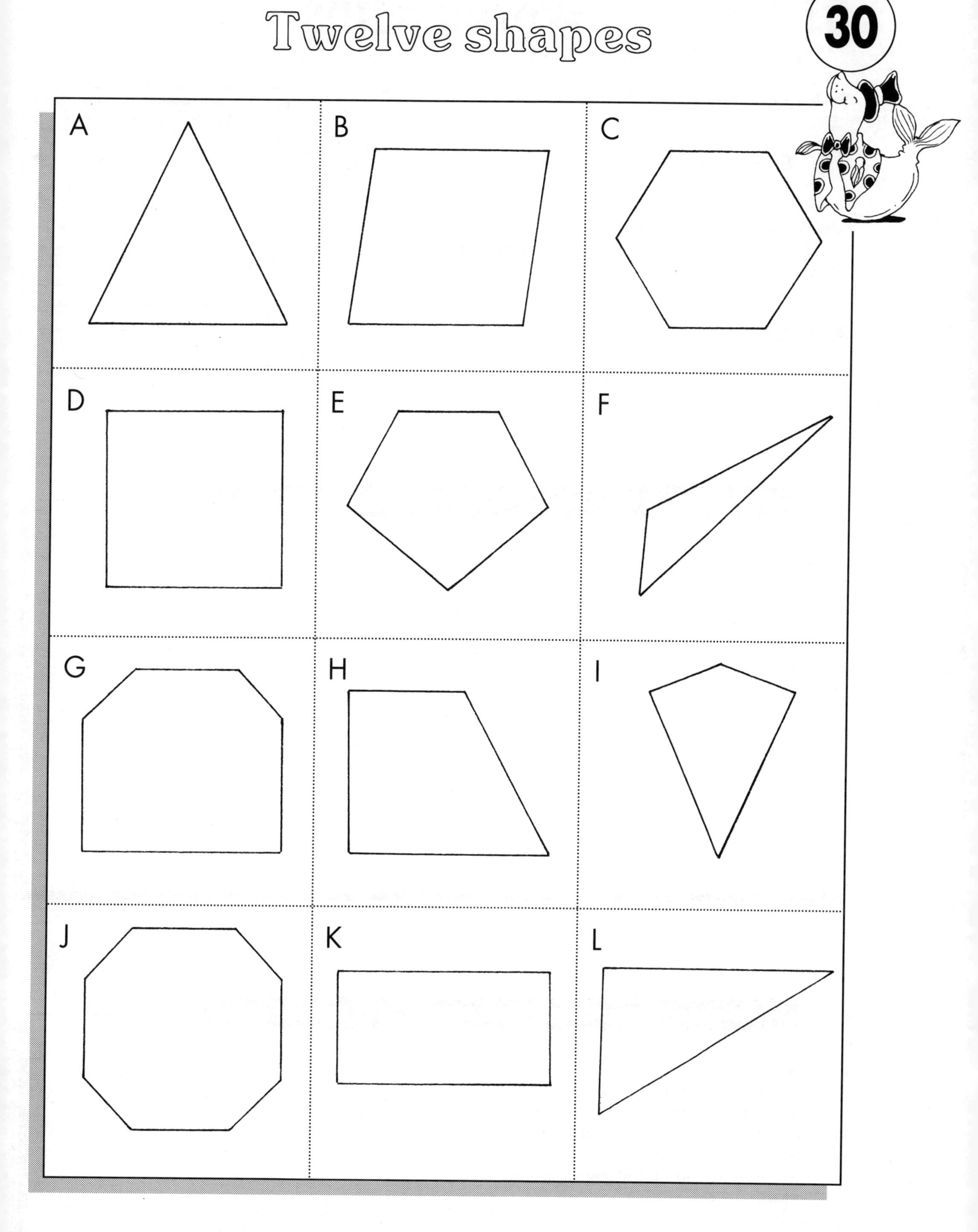

Write below each shape the number of sides it has.

31 Wordlengths

Tables

Bar graphs

Constructing a frequency table based on the number of letters (wordlength) in the words from a passage of writing. Interpreting the table. Drawing a bar graph to represent the frequency of different wordlengths.

LEVEL	Profile Component 1				Profile Component 2		
	UA	N	A	M	UA	S	D
1							
2					●		●
3					●		
4					●		●
5							
6							
7							
8							
9							
10							

D2 Frequency tables.
D3 Bar graphs.

Activity

Read through the passage and count the number of letters in each word. Construct a tally chart for the occurrence of each worldlength.

Handling the data – sample activities

- Draw a bar graph to show the frequency of wordlengths (**represent data**). Write some sentences about it (**interpret data**).
- Find five words which have two letters, three letters, four letters, ... (**process data**).
- Find one of your own pieces of writing, construct a frequency table for the wordlength, draw a graph and write about it (**using and applying; collect, process, record, represent, interpret data**).

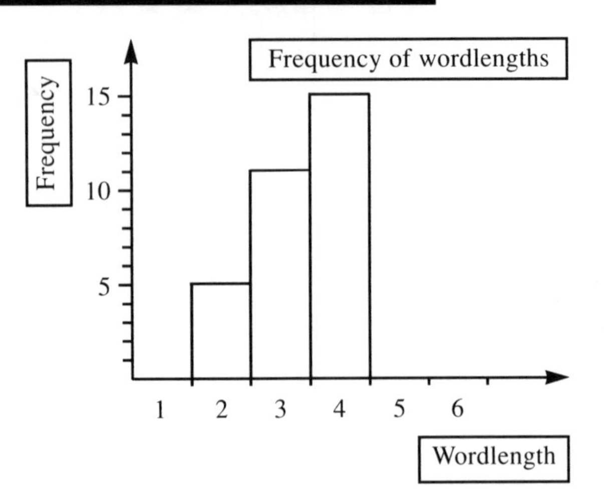

Interpreting the data – sample questions

- How many words had five letters, three letters, ...?
- Which wordlength occurred ... times?
- Which wordlength was the most common, second most common?
- Which wordlengths occurred more than five times, less than three times, ...?
- How many words had less than three letters?
- How many words had more than seven letters?

Word lengths

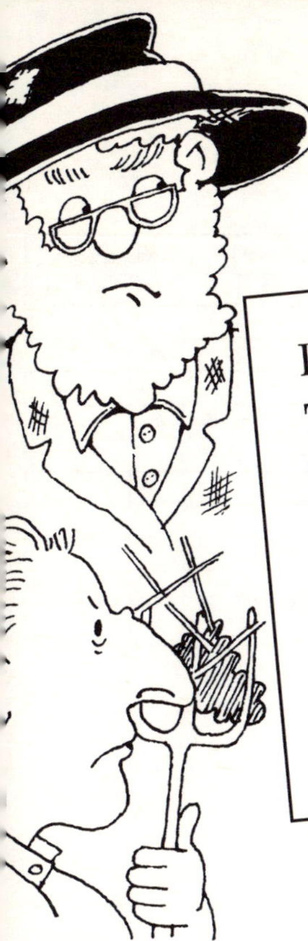

Down in the valley there were three farms. The owners of these farms had done well. They were rich men. They were also nasty men. All three of them were about as nasty and mean as any men you could meet. Their names were Farmer Boggis, Farmer Bunce and Farmer Bean.

From *Fantastic Mr Fox* by Roald Dahl (Unwin Hyman)

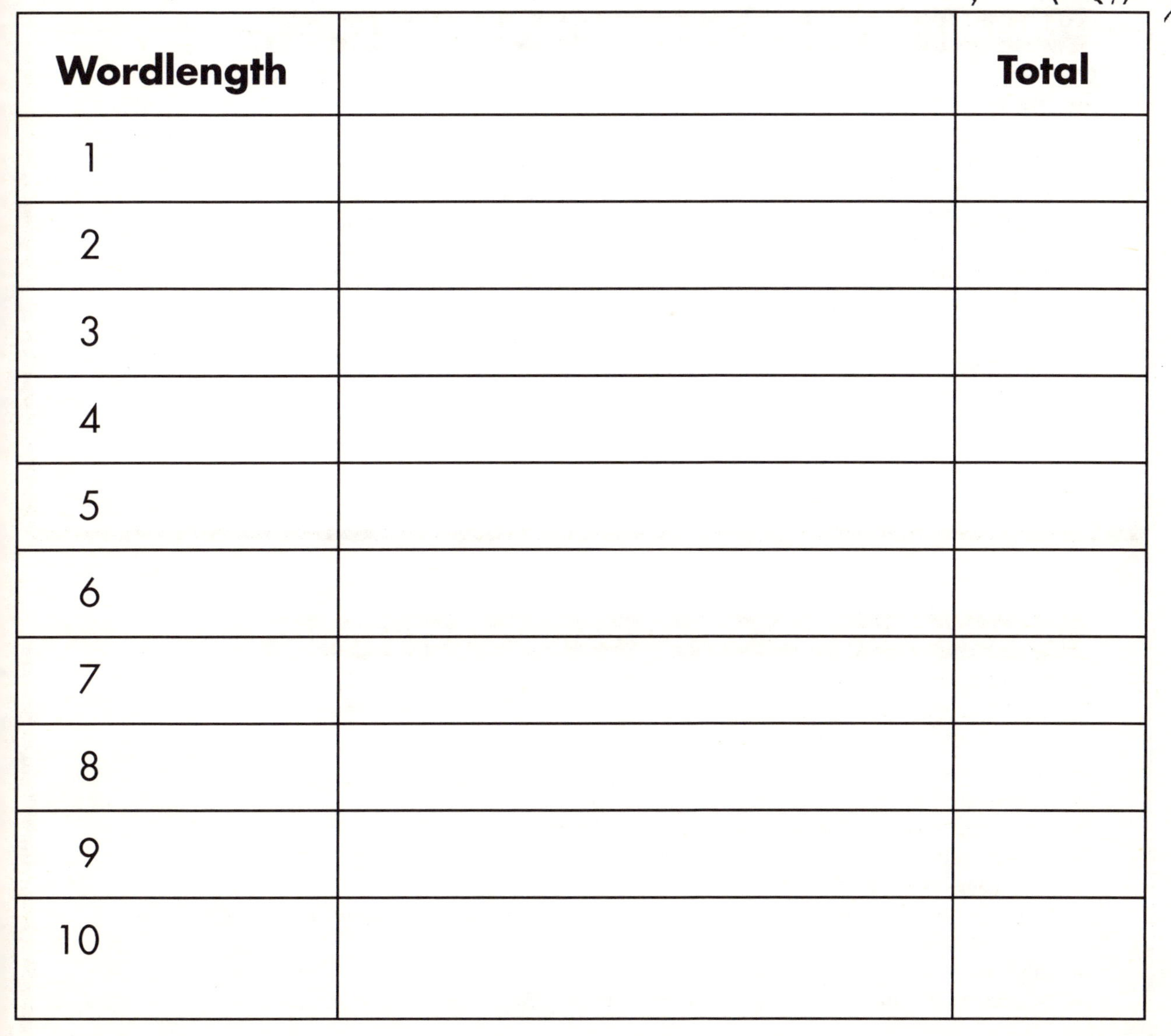

Wordlength		Total
1		
2		
3		
4		
5		
6		
7		
8		
9		
10		

32 Bus route

Tables

Bar graph

Interpreting a bus timetable and calculating the time taken for each stage of the journey. Constructing a table and drawing a bar graph to illustrate the data.

LEVEL	Profile Component 1				Profile Component 2		
	UA	N	A	M	UA	S	D
1							
2					●		
3					●		●
4				●	●		
5							
6							
7							
8							
9							
10							

M4 Reading timetables.
D3 Tables. Bar graph.

Handling the data – sample activities

- Construct a table to show how long each stage of the journey takes. (**process data**). Draw a bar graph to illustrate the time for each stage (**represent data**).
- Collect some local bus timetables and analyse them in a similar way (**using and applying; collect, process, represent, interpret data**).

Stage		Time in minutes
A	BUS STATION → HOSPITAL	11
B	HOSPITAL → CITY ROAD	17
C	CITY ROAD → HIGH STREET	8
D	HIGH STREET → RAILWAY STATION	10

Interpreting the data – sample questions

- How many bus stops are there?
- What time does the first bus leave the bus station?
- What time does it arrive at the library, the park, ...?
- What time does the last bus arrive at Wiggly Brook?
- How long does it take to get from High Street to the railway station, ...?
- How long does it take to get from the bus station to High Street, The Crown, ...?
- How long does the whole journey take?
- How long would you have to wait for the bus if you arrived at the hospital at 11.00, City Road at 2.00, ...?
- How many buses are there in a day?
- Which bus do you catch if you want to be at Wiggly Brook by 11.00, 3.00, ...?

Bus route

BUS STATION	0904	then	04	until	1600
HOSPITAL	0915	at	15		1615
CITY ROAD	0932	these	32		1632
HIGH STREET	0940	mins.	40		1640
RAILWAY STATION	0950	past	50		1650
LIBRARY	0958	each	58		1658
THE CROWN	1002	hour	02		1702
PARK	1013		13		1713
WIGGLY BROOK	1027		27		1727

How long does each stage of the route take?

33 Trays

Tables

Bar graphs

Data collection

Collection and analysis of data based on remembering a trayful of objects which are visible for a limited time-period. Constructing tables to illustrate the results.

Apparatus

A collection of objects on a tray or Spectrum Sheet 33.

LEVEL	Profile Component 1				Profile Component 2		
	UA	N	A	M	UA	S	D
1							
2							
3							●
4							
5							
6							
7							
8							
9							
10							

D3 Tables. Bar graph.

Activity

Use Spectrum Sheet 33 or place ten objects on a tray. Give a group of children one minute to look at the sheet or the tray and try to remember the objects. Remove the sheet or tray and the children write down as many objects as they can remember.

Handling the data – sample activities

- **Collect data** about which objects were remembered. Make a table to summarise the data (**process data**). Write some sentences about the table (**interpret data**).
- Repeat the activity for a different set of objects.
- Draw a bar graph to show the total number of objects remembered by each member of the group (**represent data**).

Object	Tom	Jane	Alison	Rebecca		Total
shoe	✔		✔			
pen	✔	✔	✔	✔		
ball	✔			✔		
ruler	✔	✔	✔			
Total						

Interpreting the data – sample questions

- How many objects did you remember?
- Which objects did you not remember?
- Who remembered the apple, book, ...?
- Who remembered the most objects?
- How many children remembered the ball, ruler, ...?
- Which object was remembered by everyone?
- Which object was most forgotten?

Trays

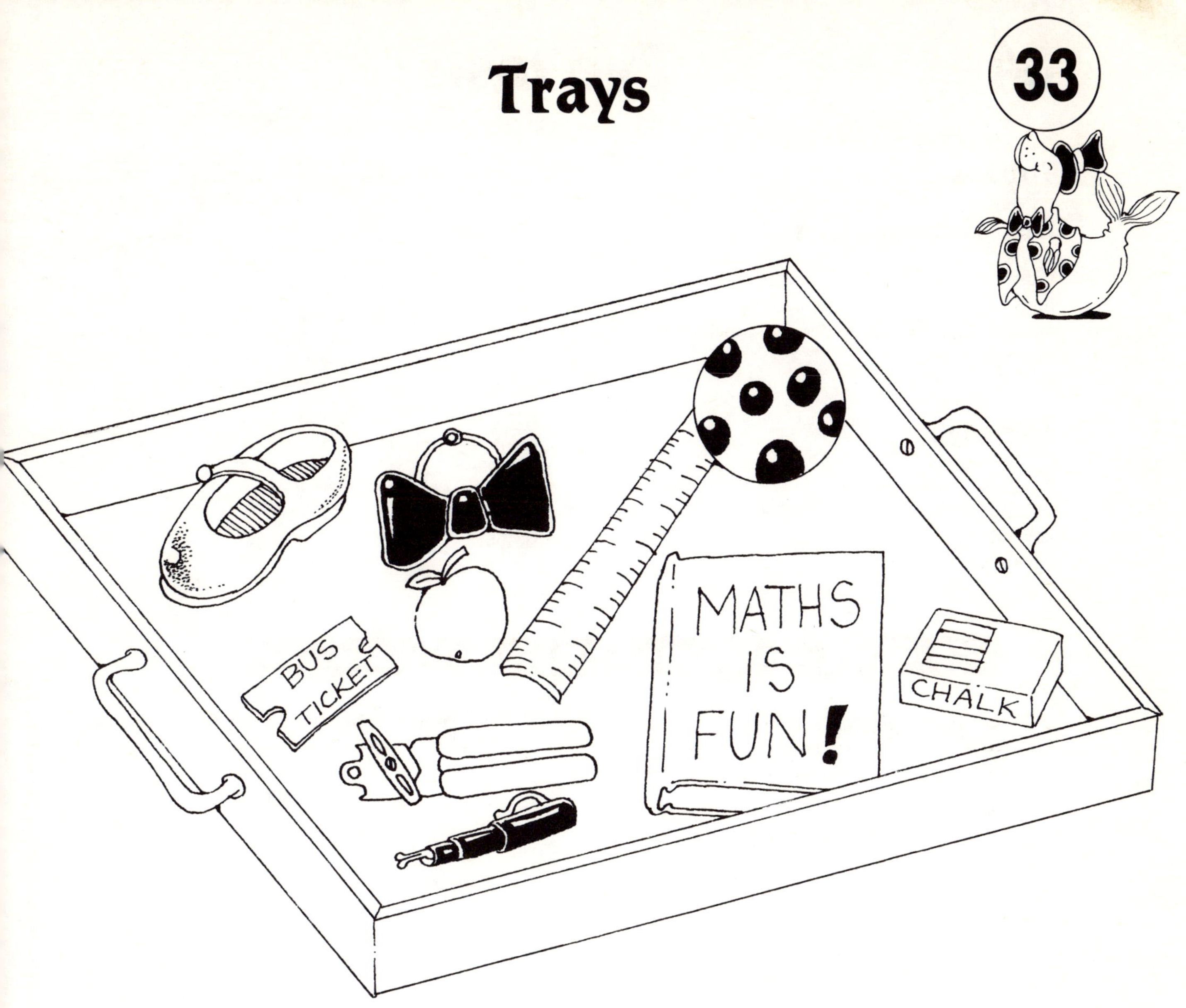

Objects

34 Eye tests

Tables

Bar line graphs

Using an eye test card to generate data based on the number of lines pupils can read whilst standing at different distances from the card. Constructing tables and drawing bar line graphs to illustrate the data.

LEVEL	Profile Component 1				Profile Component 2		
	UA	N	A	M	UA	S	D
1							
2					●		
3					●		●
4					●		●
5							
6							
7							
8							
9							
10							

D3 Tables.
D4 Bar line graphs.

Activity

Place the eye test sheet on a wall. Make some marks on the floor at 1 m 2 m, 3 m, ... away from the base of the wall. In pairs, see how many lines can be read at each mark. One person reads, the other checks.

Handling the data – sample activities

- Each pupil draws a table to show the number of lines read from different distances (**collect, process data**).
- Draw bar line graphs to illustrate the data in the table (**represent data**).
- Make some different eye test cards and experiment with left eye closed, then right eye closed. Compare the two sets of results (**using and applying; collect process, record, represent, interpret data**).
- Make some eye test cards with numbers instead of letters (**using and applying**).
- If you wear spectacles, you could record the distances for reading letters with and without glasses.

Distance in metres	Number of lines
1	8
2	7
3	5
4	5
5	3

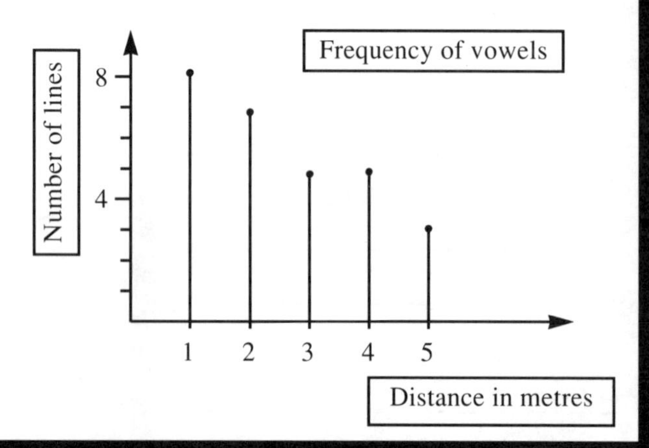

Note
This activity may be an opportunity to see whether any of your children may need a genuine eye test.

Interpreting the data – sample questions

- How many lines would you read from three metres, four metres, ...
- How far away can you stand and yet read all of the lines?
- How near do you need to be to see the bottom line, next to the bottom line, ...?
- Which is your best eye, left or right?
- How many of the lines contain an E, Z, ...?
- Which letter appears the most often?
- Which letters do not appear?

Eye tests

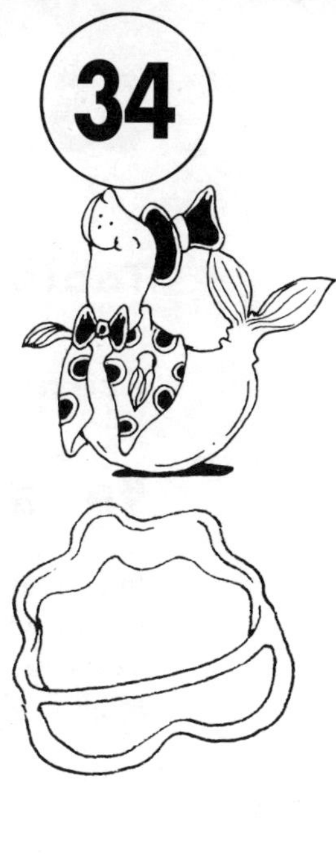

Z

D E

F H P

N V R U

Z D E F H

P E N R U Z

V Z D H P E R U

D H V E R F U P

35 Putting green

Tables

Frequency tables

Bar graphs

Interpreting a table showing the scores of three children on a putting green. Drawing bar graphs to illustrate the performance of each child on each hole. Analysing the scores and constructing a frequency table to condense the data.

LEVEL	Profile Component 1				Profile Component 2		
	UA	N	A	M	UA	S	D
1							
2					●		●
3					●		●
4					●		
5							
6							
7							
8							
9							
10							

D2 Frequency tables.
D3 Tables. Bar graphs.

Handling the data – sample activities

- Find the total scores for each player (**process data**).
- Draw a bar graph to show the number of shots taken on each hole by Mina (**represent data**). Write something about the graph (**interpret data**). Repeat for the other two players.
- Construct a frequency table to show the number of scores of 1, 2, 3, ... which occurred in the match (**process data**). Draw a graph to illustrate the results (**represent data**).
- Organise a putting competition, collect scores and analyse the data (**using and applying**).

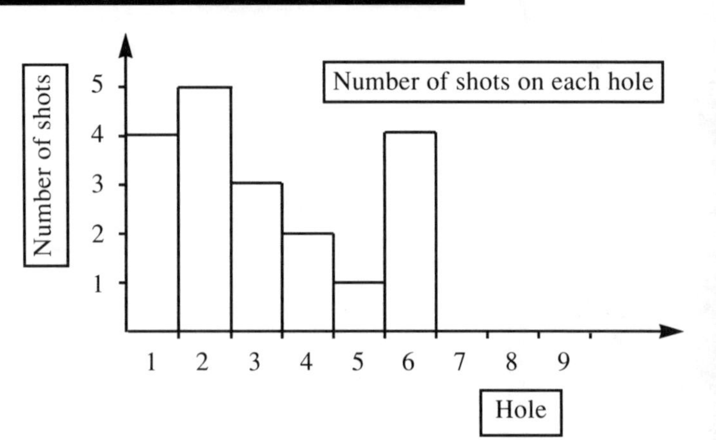

Scores		Frequency
1		
2		
3		
4		
5		
6		

Interpreting the data – sample questions

- How many holes are there on the putting green?
- How many shots did Mina take on the 1st hole, 4th hole, ...?
- At which holes did Shirley take two shots, three shots, ...?
- Which was Reuben's best hole, worst hole?
- Who performed the best on the 3rd hole, 9th hole, ...?
- How many more shots did Reuben take than Mina on the 4th hole?
- What was the total number of shots for all three players on the 8th hole, ...?
- How many times did the players take two shots, three shots, ...?

Putting green

HOLE	MINA	REUBEN	SHIRLEY
1	4	3	5
2	5	2	1
3	3	4	3
4	2	5	2
5	1	2	1
6	4	4	6
7	3	3	2
8	5	2	5
9	3	2	4

Write some sentences about these scores.

36 Two cubes

Frequency tables
Bar graphs
Chance
Data collection

Throwing two dice, each numbered 1, 1, 2, 2, 3, 3, finding the sum, recording it in a frequencey table, and then drawing a bar chart to illustrate the results.

LEVEL	Profile Component 1				Profile Component 2		
	UA	N	A	M	UA	S	D
1							
2		●			●		●
3		●			●		●
4					●		
5							
6							
7							
8							
9							
10							

N2/N3 Addition.
D2 Frequency tables.
D3 Bar graphs. Equally likely chance events.

Apparatus

Make two dice by numbering the faces of each of two cubes 1, 1, 2, 2, 3, 3.

Activity

Throw both dice several times, find the dice total and record in the table. Stop when one sum occurs with a frequency of 10.

Handling the data – sample activities

- Draw a bar graph to illustrate the frequency of each dice total (**represent data**). Write some sentences about the graph (**interpret data**).
- Repeat the activity to see if the results are the same. Compare the two graphs (**using and applying**).
- Devise another experiment by renumbering the cubes. Construct a frequency table and draw a bar graph to show the results (**using and applying; collect, record, process, represent, interpret data**).

Interpreting the data – sample questions

- Which different dice totals are possible?
- How many times did the dice total 2, 3, ... occur?
- Which dice total occurred most often, next most often, ...?
- Which dice total occurred 5 times, 8 times, ...?
- How many times was the dice total more than 4, less than 4?
- How many times was the dice total odd, even?
- How many throws were needed altogether?
- Why is it not possible to have a dice total of 7, 1, ...?

Two cubes

Make two dice by numbering the faces of each of two cubes 1, 1, 2, 2, 3, 3.

Dice total		Frequency

Frequency of dice totals

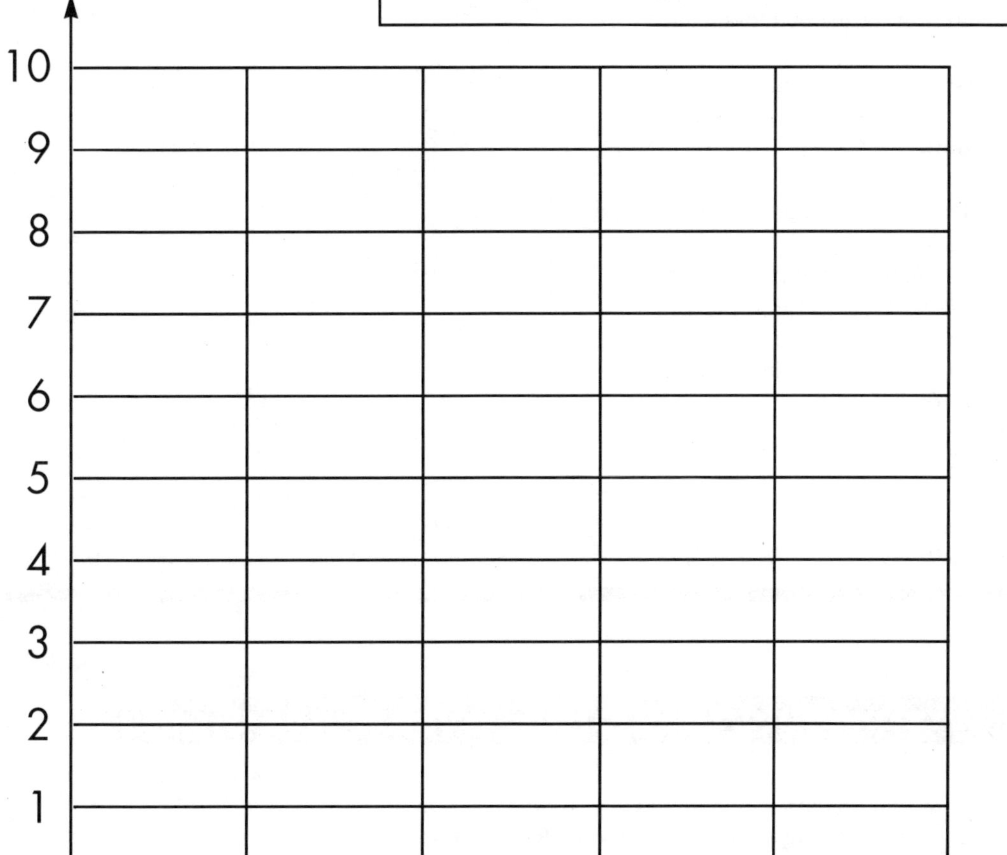

Frequency

Dice total

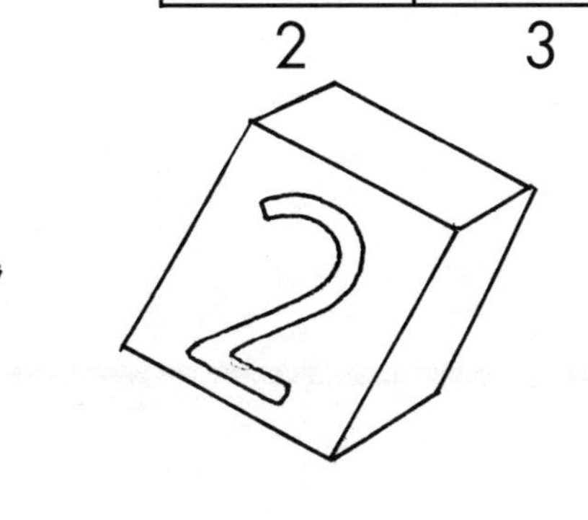

more
DATA HANDLING
SPECTRUM MATHS

37 Picture gallery

Tables

Constructing a table to detail the type and dimension of sets of squares and rectangles. Areas of squares and rectangles by counting squares. Drawing a set of different squares and rectangles.

LEVEL	Profile Component 1				Profile Component 2		
	UA	N	A	M	UA	S	D
1							
2					●	●	
3					●		●
4				●	●		
5							
6							
7							
8							
9							
10							

M4 Areas by counting squares
S2 Recognise squares and retangles
D3 Tables.

Handling the data – sample activities

- Construct a table to show the different shapes (**process data**). Repeat for the bottom picture.
- Make a list putting the pictures in order of size of area (**process data**).
- Draw your own picture containing squares and rectangles, letter them, and then draw a table to list the shapes, their sides, and their areas (**using and applying; process data**).

For example: top picture

	Shape	Sides	Squares filled
A	RECTANGLE	2, 4	8
B	SQUARE	4, 4	16
C	RECTANGLE	2, 6	12
D	RECTANGLE	2, 3	6
E	RECTANGLE	2, 1	2
F	SQUARE	3, 3	9
G	RECTANGLE	3, 1	3
H	RECTANGLE	2, 6	12

	Shape	Sides	Area
B	SQUARE	4, 4	16
C	RECTANGLE	2, 6	12
H	RECTANGLE	2, 6	12

Interpreting the data – sample questions

- How many shapes in the top picture, bottom picture?
- Which shapes are squares in the top picture, bottom picture?
- Which shapes in each picture are rectangles?
- Which shapes have a side of length 2 units, 3 units, ...?
- Which shapes fill exactly 6 squares, 4 squares, ...?
- Which shape fills the most squares, next most squares, ...?
- Which is the biggest picture at the top, at the bottom?
- Which is the smallest picture at the bottom, ...?
- Which pictures are the same size?

Picture gallery

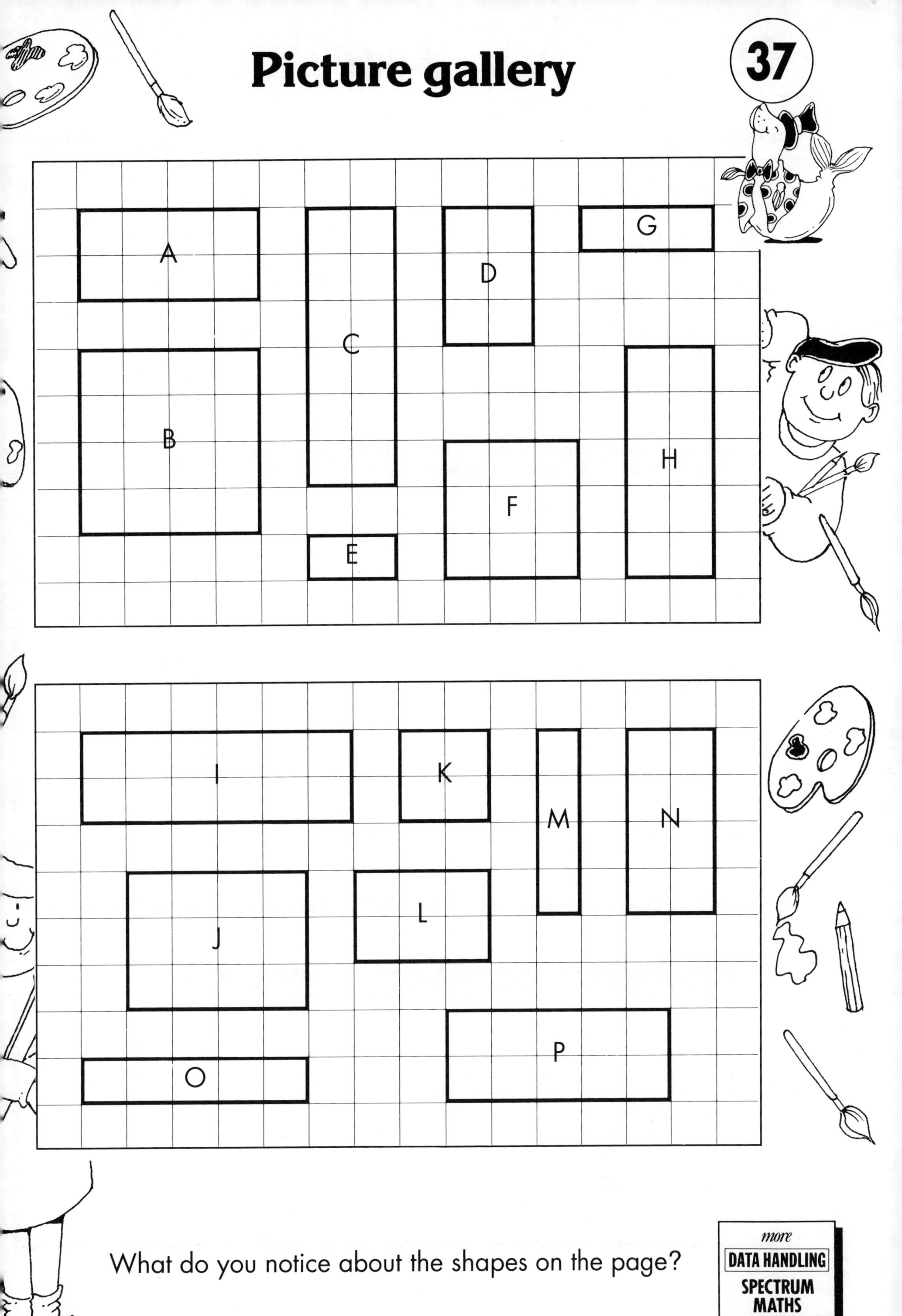

What do you notice about the shapes on the page?

more DATA HANDLING SPECTRUM MATHS

Eggs

Lists

Frequency tables

Bar graphs

Data collection

Analysing a set of data relating to thirty children's preferences for methods of cooking eggs. Constructing frequency tables, drawing bar graphs and collection of data based on class' preferences.

LEVEL	Profile Component 1				Profile Component 2		
	UA	N	A	M	UA	S	D
1							
2					●		●
3					●		●
4					●		
5							
6							
7							
8							
9							
10							

D2 Frequency tables. Data collection.
D3 Bar graphs. Lists.

Handling the data – sample activities

- Construct a frequency table to show the distribution of children's preferences (**process data**).

		Total
BOILED	~~||||~~ ||||	9
FRIED	~~||||~~ ~~||||~~ ||	12
POACHED	|||	3
SCRAMBLED	~~||||~~		6

- Draw a bar graph to illustrate the data in the table (**represent data**). Write some sentences about the table (**interpret data**).
- **Collect data** from pupils in the class on their choice of egg preference and analyse it in a similar way (**using and applying**).

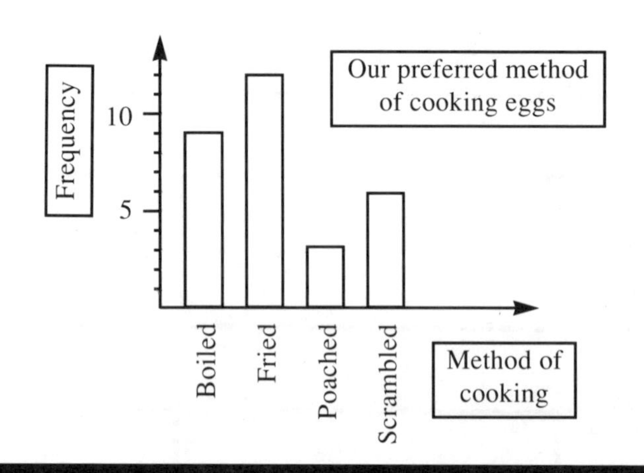

Interpreting the data – sample questions

- How do Salito, Phil, Lucy, ... like their eggs cooked?
- Who likes their eggs scrambled?
- How many children are there altogether?
- How many voted for fried, boiled, ...?
- How many more voted for scrambled than poached?
- Which was the most popular method of cooking eggs for these children?
- What is your preference?

Eggs

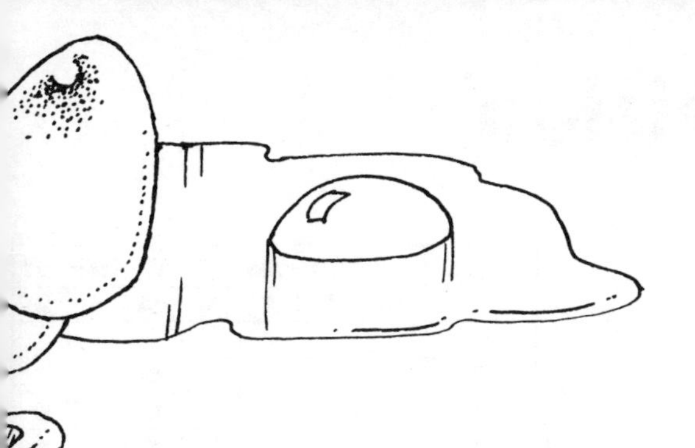

BOILED POACHED SCRAMBLED FRIED

How we like our eggs cooked

Katie	BOILED	**Hamid**	SCRAMBLED
Judith	SCRAMBLED	**Maura**	FRIED
Shaun	FRIED	**James**	BOILED
Dean	FRIED	**Chetan**	FRIED
Olenka	POACHED	**Sharon**	FRIED
Elroy	FRIED	**Louise**	POACHED
Samantha	BOILED	**Debbie**	BOILED
Damian	BOILED	**Leroy**	FRIED
Ashish	FRIED	**Maria**	POACHED
Salito	FRIED	**Andrew**	BOILED
Karen	SCRAMBLED	**Phil**	FRIED
Kelly	BOILED	**Rabab**	SCRAMBLED
Sue	SCRAMBLED	**David**	BOILED
Spiro	BOILED	**Lucy**	FRIED
Tracey	FRIED	**Gobind**	SCRAMBLED

Write some sentences about this information.

39 Third division

Lists

Bar line graph

Data collection

Analysis of a list of football statistics in terms of the attendance figures in thousands. Drawing a bar line graph to illustrate the figures.

LEVEL	Profile Component 1				Profile Component 2		
	UA	N	A	M	UA	S	D
1							
2					●		
3		●			●		●
4					●		●
5							
6							
7							
8							
9							
10							

N3 Ordering numbers up to 10 000.
D3 Lists.
D4 Bar line graphs.

Handling the data – sample activities

- Draw a bar line graph to show the attendances at each match (**represent data**). Write some sentences about it (**interpret data**).
- **Collect data** regarding attendances at football matches from the Sunday newspapers and analyse the figures (**using and applying**).

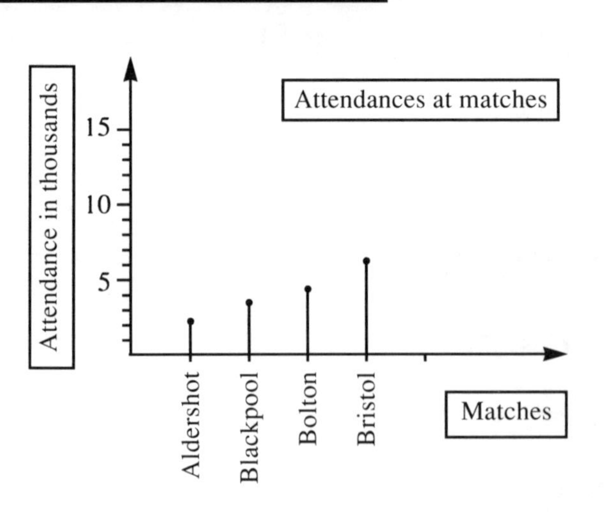

Interpreting the data – sample questions

- What was the attendance at Port Vale, Fulham, ...?
- Which matches had an attendance of 4000, ...?
- Which match had the highest, lowest attendance?
- How many matches had an attendance greater than 8000, less than 5000, between 3000 and 7000?
- How many more people watched the match at Wolves than at Northampton?
- What was the total attendance at all of the matches?
- Which teams scored 4 goals, 2 goals, ...?
- Which game produced the most goals, fewest goals, ...?

Third division

FOOTBALL RESULTS

SATURDAY MARCH 18TH

				Attendance
ALDERSHOT	2	CHESTERFIELD	0	2,000
BLACKPOOL	1	CHESTER	1	3,000
BOLTON	0	SOUTHEND	0	4,000
BRISTOL CITY	0	NOTTS COUNTY	4	6,000
FULHAM	2	CARDIFF	0	4,000
NORTHAMPTON	2	MANSFIELD	1	3,000
PORT VALE	1	PRESTON	1	9,000
SHEFFIELD UNITED	1	READING	0	12,000
WOLVES	4	BURY	0	15,000

Write about the attendances at these football matches.

more DATA HANDLING SPECTRUM MATHS

40 Our weights

Group frequency table (continuous)

Group frequency diagram (continuous)

Data collection

Measuring the weights in kg of each pupil. Constructing a group frequency table to condense the data and drawing a group frequency diagram to illustrate the results.

LEVEL	Profile Component 1				Profile Component 2		
	UA	N	A	M	UA	S	D
1							
2					●		
3				●	●		
4					●		
5							●
6							
7							
8							
9							
10							

M3 Measuring weight.
D5 Group frequency tables. Group frequency diagrams (continuous data).

Activity

Use a set of bathroom scales to measure the pupils' weights.

Handling the data – sample activities

- Record the weights with tally marks in the group frequency table on the sheet (**record data**), then draw a group frequency diagram (**represent data**). Write some sentences about the graph (**interpret data**).
- **Collect data** for another class, construct a table, draw a diagram, compare and write about it (**using and applying; process, record, represent, interpret data**).
- Measure the weights of teachers and other adults. Construct an appropriate group frequency table, then draw a group frequency diagram. Write about it (**using and applying**).

Interpreting the data – sample questions

- How many pupils' weight is in the 35–40 kg, 40–45 kg, ... group?
- Which group is the most common, next most common, ...?
- Are there any groups with no entries?
- Do you need any extra groups?
- Which groups contain more than four pupils, less than three pupils, ...?
- How many pupils weigh more than 40 kg, less than 35 kg, between 35 and 45 kg, ...?

Our weights

Weight in kg		Frequency
20–25		
26–30		
30–35		
36–40		
40–45		
46–50		
50–55		
56–60		

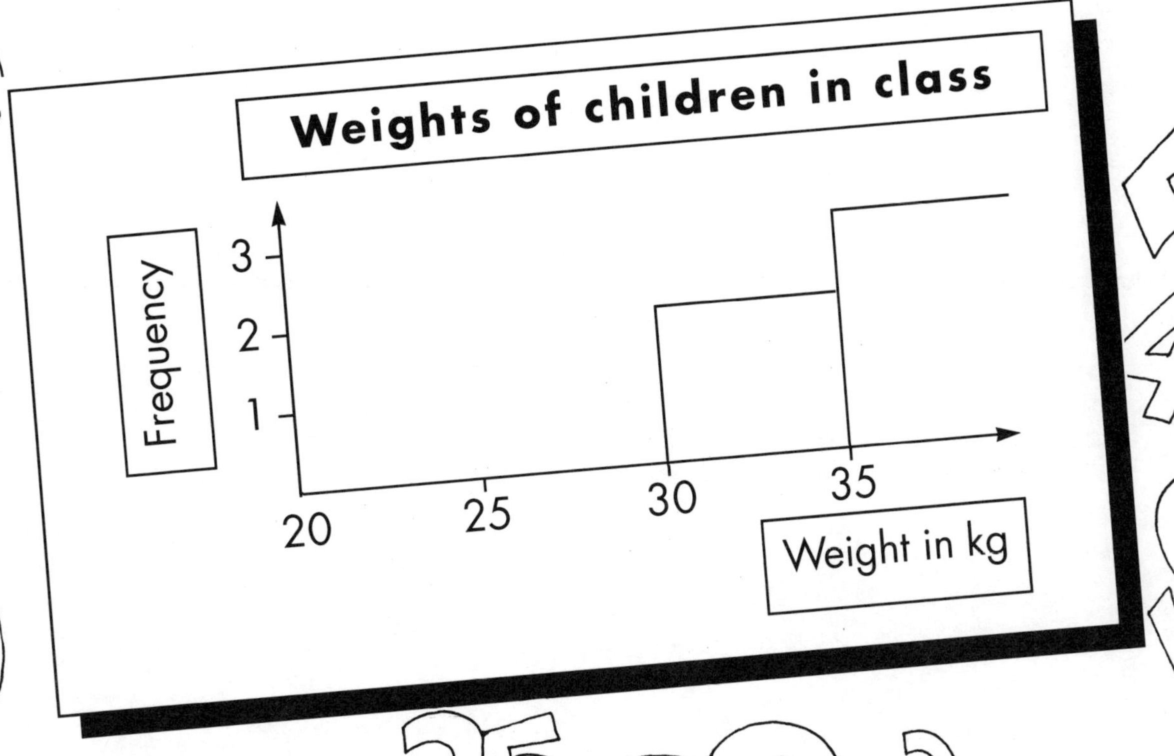

Some suggested software which may be useful for 'Handling data'

Key Stage 1 and 2

Our Facts *Branch* *Notice Board*	NCET University of Warwick

Key Stage 2 and 3

Junior Find	RESOURCE, Exeter Road, Doncaster DN2 4PY
Grass *Grasshopper*	Newman College, Garners Lane, Bartley Green, Birmingham B32 3NT

Spectrum Maths

The **Spectrum Maths Data Handling** series is a valuable addition to the other **Spectrum Maths** material. Namely: